Jacinta

The Flower of Fatima

Jacinta
The Flower of Fatima

By

HUMBERTO SOUSA MEDEIROS

With a Foreword by
FULTON J. SHEEN, D.D.

TAN Books

Charlotte, North Carolina

Cum Permissu Superiorum.

Nihil Obstat: JOHN M. FEARNS, S.T.D.,
 Censor Librorum.

Imprimatur: † FRANCIS CARDINAL SPELLMAN,
 Archbishop of New York.

August 15, 1946.
Feast of the Assumption.

Jacinta: The Flower of Fatima by Rev. Humberto S. Medeiros and Rev. William F. Hill. Arranged from the Portuguese of Rev. Joseph Galamba de Oliveira. This book was first published in 1946 by Catholic Book Publishing Co. New York, NY. This TAN Books edition has been re-typeset and revised to include corrections of typographical errors and updating of punctuation, spelling and diction. *Jacinta: The Flower of Fatima* © 2017 TAN Books. All rights reserved.

Cover design by Tarina Weese
Cover image Public domain via Wikimedia Commons

ISBN: 978-1-50511-103-3

Printed and bound in the United States of America.

TAN Books
Charlotte, North Carolina
www.TANBooks.com
2017

To the memory of
Father Anthony Vieban, S.S.
beloved priest and teacher, who in his own life went,
and taught his students to go, "To Jesus, through Mary."

Declaration

In accordance with the decrees of Urban VIII, we declare that in speaking of the events, prodigies and miracles of Fatima, we wish to speak of them in the sense in which the Ecclesiastical Authority approved them on October 13, 1930, without desiring in any way to anticipate the decision of the Holy See.

Contents

Publisher's Note

We here at TAN are very pleased in this centennial anniversary year of the apparitions at Fatima to present to our readers this charming volume on Jacinta Marto, now St. Jacinta. While certain minor updates have been made to the original English version first published in 1946, we have chosen not to change any of the text with regards to dating from the time of the apparition, nor to insert any changes with regards to what has been learned about the apparition or historical events—such as the recent canonization of Jacinta and Francisco—in the intervening years. While certainly a great part of the charm of the book lies in its descriptions of the home and pastoral life of Jacinta—often relayed through the first-person testimony of Lucia— equally valuable, and interesting we believe, is the opportunity to see how those events were viewed through a mid-twentieth-century lens. We hope you agree and that you enjoy and benefit from this book as much as we have.

Translator's Note

The apparitions of the Mother of God at Fatima, Portugal, have aroused great interest among the Catholic population of our country. Already several articles and pamphlets have been published describing the visions of the three little shepherds. The message which the Heavenly Mother brought to mankind twenty-nine years ago has excited the wonder and devotion of many a Christian soul. Its inner meaning, however, was hidden from us until the miracle of grace wrought in the souls of the three privileged children was made known. The story of the life of little Jacinta Marto the youngest of the seers leads us, in the words of the Cardinal Patriarch of Lisbon, "into the heart of Fatima." It is a letter from the Blessed Virgin to be read with the eyes of the soul.

THE TRANSLATORS.
Theological College,
Catholic University of America,
May, 1946.

"She said that she was *Our Lady of the Rosary;* that *we must repent of our sins, change our life, offend Our Lord no more, because He is offended too much; and that we must say our rosary.*"

Foreword

The measure of God's judgment of the world at any given period of history is the size of the Saints he sends to regenerate it. When there was a genuine humility among men, God sent intellectual giants like Thomas, Bonaventure, and Albert. Now that there is a pride about human knowledge, God sends children. The outstanding Saints of the modern world have been Father John Vianney, the Curé of Ars, who barely made the grades necessary for ordination; Saint Theresa, the Little Flower, who chose the way of spiritual childhood. Our Lady revealed herself to a little peasant girl at Lourdes, who had never heard of the Immaculate Conception, and more lately at Fatima the Blessed Mother gave her revelation to three little children, Lúcia, aged 11, Jacinta, aged 7, and Francisco, aged 9.

Thus there seems to be verified in this generation what the self-wise Corinthians learned was God's high manner under these conditions: "But the foolish things of the world hath God chosen that He may confound the wise, and the weak things of the world hath God chosen that he may confound the strong." (I Cor. 1, 27). As man exalts himself, God humiliates him. The Son of God was born in a cave, and the peculiar quality about every cave is that in order to enter you must stoop, and the stoop is the stoop of humility. Proud men refuse to stoop and miss the vision of a Babe Whose tiny hands were not quite long enough to touch the huge heads of the cattle, and yet they were hands that held within their fingers the reins that steer the sun, moon and stars in their courses.

Only two classes of people found the Child: the Wise Men and the Shepherds; those who know they do not know everything and those who know they know nothing. Never the man that thinks he knows. "O Heavenly Father, I thank thee that thou hast hidden these things from the wise and prudent, and revealed them to the little ones."

In an age which boasts of its omniscience God chooses to drive it in nescience by sending little people, with little minds but with great understanding; little flowers but with deep burning centers; little children who know nothing about politics to discourse on the significance of two world wars in 21 years.

This particular book is the story of one of God's little giants, Jacinta, who was wise beyond all learning, for who is not wise when instructed by heaven? She reveals to our world which trusts in power that though heaven's gates are resistant to the smiting of mighty hands, they nevertheless swing open to the gentle touch of a child. Heaven is not available to the aged: no old people can enter in. "Unless you become as little children, you shall not enter the Kingdom of Heaven." (Matt., 18, 3)

One day as the Apostle strove for the Presidency and Vice-Presidency of the Kingdom, Our Lord put a child in the midst of them—St. Mark says He took the child in His arms—and then spoke the words above about becoming little. Only in the presence of its opposite does a vice feel shame.

But the childlikeness which is necessary for entrance into heaven and for understanding sublime truths of faith is not the same as childishness. Our Lord in exalting the child was not blessing imperfection or mediocrity, saplings or lambs. He was rather taking the swank air of superiority. What makes social life dull is its group of proud who always want to stand at the head of the line and be the first in. But when God looks out from high heaven to choose instruments for his message to the world, He starts at the other end of the queue. He does this because the adults of the world can learn to love again in no better way than through children who break open the wells of love and keep them flowing over arid wastes. Remake man and you remake the world, but to remake man means to become as a child. "You must be born again." Jacinta is such a model, for she never once roused herself to be humble. Humility flowed from her as naturally as water bubbles from a spring. Sought childlikeness is artificiality. Childlikeness inspired by love betrays one who heard: "Learn of me, for I am meek and humble of heart." Maybe there are only nurseries in Heaven!

MONSIGNOR FULTON J. SHEEN, D.D.
Catholic University of America,
Feast of the Annunciation, 1946.

JACINTA FRANCISCO LUCIA

Prologue

For the sake of completeness and clarity it was thought advisable to introduce the story of Jacinta's life to our American readers with a brief account of the marvelous events which have made an obscure mountain village a place of worldwide renown and the goal of numberless pilgrimages.

Fatima lies about one hundred miles north of Lisbon, Portugal, in the mountain country of the diocese of Leiria. In 1917 it did not number more than 2,600 souls, most of whom lived from their lands and flocks. On May 13 of that year three little shepherd children were watching over their sheep in the Cova da Iria. They were Jacinta, a little girl of seven, Francisco, her nine-year-old brother, and their cousin, Lúcia Santos, a girl of ten. They could neither read nor write, but they had been taught their prayers and knew their catechism, and Lúcia had made her First Communion.

The Prologue has been taken from the "Miracle of Fatima" by Rev. João da Cruz, C.S.Sp., translated by Rev. Robert L. Heim, C.S.Sp.

The First Apparition

At noon they prepared to say the rosary as was their custom. Suddenly a great flash of light rent the sky. The children, looking up, could not see the vestige of a cloud, but thought perhaps a storm was gathering behind the mountain. Somewhat frightened, they decided to return home as quickly as possible, and descended the slope, driving the sheep before them. On reaching the foot of the hill they were brought to a halt by a second flash of light more brilliant than the first. Speechless with wonder and trembling from unexplained emotion, all three, moved by a common impulse, looked toward the right.

There, standing on the branches of a small green oak, a few feet away, was a beautiful Lady, glorious and resplendent as the sun.[1] Dazzled and half-blinded, the children were seized with fright and started to run away; but the Apparition, with a gesture which bespoke motherly tenderness, said to them, "Be not afraid! I am not going to hurt you." Awe-struck, they stood gazing on this lovely Vision.

---

1 This was not the first heavenly apparition which the children experienced. The Story of Jacinta reveals for the first time that a year before the first apparition of Our Lady, the Angel of Portugal had appeared to them. *Cf.* chapter 8, page 70.

The Lady seemed about sixteen or eighteen years of age and was clothed in a white gown gathered at the neck with a gold cord. A white veil embroidered with gold covered her head and shoulders and, like the gown, reached to her feet, which were scarcely visible as they rested on the branches of the tree. She stood in an attitude of prayer, her hands joined at her breast, while in her right hand she held a rosary of brilliant pearls from which hung a silver cross. Her face, indescribably beautiful, shone radiantly in a halo of sunlight, yet was shadowed by a veil of sadness.

Several minutes of ecstatic silence elapsed before Lúcia found courage to ask, "Where did you come from?"

"I came from heaven," replied the Vision.

"From heaven!" exclaimed Lúcia, "and why did you come here?"

"I came to ask you to come here for six successive months, on the 13th of each month, at this same hour. In October I shall tell you who I am and what it is I wish."

Gaining confidence, Lúcia continued: "You came from heaven! Will I go to heaven?"

"Yes," was the answer, "you will go to heaven, but you must say the rosary and *say it with devotion.*"

"And Jacinta?"

"Jacinta too."

"And Francisco?"

The Vision looked at the little boy with motherly reproach and answered, "He also, but he will have to say many rosaries! Are you willing to offer yourselves to God and suffer as He wishes?"

The children promised.

"And the two little girls who recently died in the village?"

"One of them is in heaven," said the Lady, "the other is still in purgatory."

Then, before leaving, the Lady said, "Always say the rosary with devotion." Whereupon, not seeming to walk but rather to glide, she turned to the east and disappeared in the light of the sun.

The Second Apparition—
The Secrets

One month later, Wednesday, June 13, the three children, followed by about sixty curious persons, arrived before noon to keep their appointment with the Lady. Climbing up the hill to the place where they had seen the flash of light, they knelt and devoutly recited the rosary. When it was finished, Lúcia arose, tidied her dress, and turned toward the east to await the "Beautiful Lady."

Those present asked, "Will she be late?"

"No," answered the girl.

The other two children were still insisting that they should say another rosary, when Lúcia, making a quick gesture of surprise, cried, "Wait, I see the light now. The Lady is coming!" Followed by the others she ran to the foot of the hill to the little green oak tree of the first apparition and there again stood the Lady.

"What do you want me to do?" asked Lúcia.

The vision answered by exhorting them to say the rosary often, adding, "After the Gloria Patri of each decade, you will say, *'O my Jesus, forgive us our sins! Save us from the fires of hell! and lead all souls to heaven, especially those who most need your mercy.'*"

Then, turning toward Lúcia, the Lady said to her, "I want you to learn to read."

After that the Lady communicated a secret for each child, commanding that what she said was to be revealed to no one. Then she withdrew in the same manner as before. Their conversation had lasted ten minutes.

Francisco, who could not hear what the Lady said, had his secret imparted to him by the girls.

Those who were present had heard what Lúcia said, but they had failed to see or hear the Lady. They had, however, been struck by the fact that, during the apparition, the noonday sun lost its brilliance and the atmosphere took on a yellow hue. Furthermore, all the buds on the green oak tree were bent toward the east, the direction in which the Lady had departed.

The Third Apparition—
Promise of a Miracle

As she had done at a previous appearance, the Lady, in the apparition of July 13, again urged the recitation of the rosary as a means of bringing the war (World War I) to an end, saying that *only through the intercession of the Blessed Virgin* could this be brought about, for *she alone can help us.*

Little Lúcia asked her, first, to say who she was and, secondly, to perform a miracle to prove the validity of the apparitions which only the children were privileged to see.

The Lady answered, "Continue to come here on the 13th of each month, and on October 13 I shall tell you who I am and what I wish, and I shall perform a *great* miracle so that all the world may believe in the apparitions."

A crowd of 5,000 heard the child speak, but were themselves unable to see or hear what was taking place. Once more everyone affirmed that, while the vision lasted, the sun lost its brilliance and the atmosphere took on a golden hue.

The Fourth Apparition—
Arrest of the children

All this, naturally, was beginning to cause a considerable sensation throughout the land. Discussions were carried on in the press, and little else was talked about but Fatima. Consequently, a great many people decided to go and see for themselves, and on Monday, August 13, some 18,000 people were en route to Fatima. They came from all directions, on foot, on bicycles, in carriages, and in cars. A number were admittedly unbelievers and came solely from curiosity, but the great majority were believers who prayed, sang hymns, and fervently said the rosary. The little oak where the Vision appeared was quickly despoiled of its leaves and branches; even bits of the bark were torn from the trunk by the eager crowd who wanted souvenirs.

Noon came and passed, but the children did not come. The people were puzzled; some became impatient, asking why they had to wait like this.

At last, word was passed around that the little ones were not coming because they had been put in jail by the Administrator of Ourém. Indignation ran through the crowd; they even threatened to go to the Administrator's house and protest against the arrest of these three harmless children.

But just then something happened for which they had not dared to hope, and their anger was forgotten. From the clear, limpid sky a clap of thunder resounded, and a brilliant light visible to all shone near the green oak of the apparitions. The sun paled and the sky turned yellow. Simultaneously an ethereal cloud, of great beauty, formed close to the oak, slowly rose in the air and disappeared. The crowd, breathless at witnessing these marvelous signs, began to cry out that it was a miracle. On leaving this favored spot, their anger was calmed and they talked of the happening, expressing the opinion that the Administrator, in keeping the children away, was opposing the Divine Will and risking the punishment of heaven.

Upon returning home from Ourém, the children had no thought of going to Cova da Iria. Since they had been prevented by force from keeping their appointment of August 13, they did not expect to see the Beautiful Lady again until September 13.

But on Sunday, August 19, at a place called Valinhos, they were greatly surprised to be favored with an apparition. The Lady expressed displeasure at their being prevented from keeping the appointment of the 13th at Cova da Iria. And she added that because of it the miracle promised for October 13 would be less remarkable than it would otherwise have been.

Lúcia asked her, "What should be done with the money and other offerings that the people left by the green oak?"

The Lady answered, "It should be used to buy two small litters for carrying statues in processions. One of them is to be carried by you, Lúcia, and three other little girls, all to be dressed in white. The other is to be carried by Francisco and three other boys, also to be dressed in white. The rest of the money should be used for the Feast of Our Lady of the Rosary, and toward the building of a chapel."

This apparition lasted the usual time and the children said farewell to the Heavenly Lady until September 13.

The Fifth Apparition

The inquest of the Administrator, far from extorting from the three children proof that the whole affair was a sham, succeeded rather in establishing their perfect sincerity and their courage in bearing witness to the supernatural. Then, too, such wonderful things had been witnessed by the crowd of 18,000 that the miracles were soon known throughout the length and breadth of the land. The final result was to dispel all doubt as to the children's honesty and to strengthen belief in the reality of the marvelous events that were taking place at Fatima. At the apparition of September 13 the influx of visitors was larger than ever, despite the fact that it was then harvest time, with work in the fields pressing.

An eyewitness records the events of that day: "On the previous day, September 12, I saw an endless stream of people coming from great distances on foot, their steps directed toward Fatima, in order to be present at the apparition the next day. I was deeply moved, and more than once tears came to my eyes when I saw the devotion, the prayerfulness, and the ardent faith of so many thousands of pilgrims, who were reciting the rosary as they walked along. The roads and bypaths were crowded with people. This was a pilgrimage truly deserving of the name. Never in my life had I witnessed so profound, so poignant a manifestation of faith. In the evening a car came into our village filled with persons who had come a great distance. They stopped there for the night and went on to Fatima the next morning. I eagerly accepted an invitation to ride with them, and we arrived about ten o'clock. Already a large crowd had gathered near the place of the visions. The men took off their hats, and almost everyone knelt and prayed fervently. There must have been 30,000 persons present before noon.

"A short time before that hour the three children arrived. Little Lúcia called out to the crowd, 'We must pray!'

"Never shall I forget," continues this witness, "the overwhelming sensation I experienced at seeing so many people, at the sound of a child's voice, fall on their knees and pray with tears in their eyes, imploring with confidence the maternal protection of the Queen of Heaven."

The sun, which had been shining brilliantly all morning, at exactly twelve noon began to lose its brightness, while the sky became a golden yellow. There was not a cloud in the heavens. The

entire crowd silently contemplated this phenomenon which had occurred on the 13th of each
month since the first apparition in May.

Until now the clergy had prudently kept away
from the demonstrations. But this time, due to the
uneasiness of the Administrator and the increas-
ing enthusiasm of the people, the Vicar General
of the diocese decided to go to Fatima on September 13 to see what would happen there. He went
incognito, taking with him another priest who was
a friend. Both were in civilian dress, and chose a
spot on the hillside a little apart from the crowd,
to watch developments. This is the authorized
account of the Vicar General:

"The crowd prayed continually until sudden
cries of surprise and joy were heard. Then thousands of arms were raised, pointing to a spot in the
sky, and cries arose of 'There! There she is! She is
coming! There, don't you see? O yes, I see!'

"I, too, looked in the direction indicated. The
priest with me said, not without a touch of mal-
ice, 'So, you are going to look too?' To my great
astonishment I saw clearly and distinctly a globe
of light advancing from east to west, gliding slowly
and majestically across the heavens. I made a sign
with my hand to this friend who was making fun

of me. Then he, too, looked up and had the consolation of witnessing this unexpected and striking phenomenon.

"Near the oak stood Lúcia, who interrupted her rosary to cry out joyously, 'Oh, there she is! She is coming! She is coming!' And indeed everyone could clearly see the luminous globe slowly advancing.

"Just then I lost sight of it, as did the priest at my side. But the little ten-year-old girl near me kept crying joyously, 'I still see her! I still see!' and thereupon ran toward the green oak."

It was the fifth apparition of the Heavenly Lady to the little shepherds of Fatima. While it was in progress, all present saw a thin, white cloud form and envelop the tree and the children. Then something still more wonderful occurred, for from the serene and cloudless sky white flowers began to fall, but, as snow-flakes sometimes do, they disappeared before reaching the earth and the waiting people. This phenomenon has been attested to and confirmed by reliable persons, including the Bishop of the diocese, who was present on another occasion when it happened, and gave witness to the fact.

All this time the crowd realized that the children were talking with an invisible being. They could hear what Lúcia said, but could not see the Lady nor hear her answers.

The Lady again impressed on the children the necessity of saying the rosary faithfully to bring about the end of the war. She promised to return on October 13 with Saint Joseph and the Infant Jesus . . . and *impressed* on the children that *they must come without fail on that date.*

Little Lúcia again asked the Lady if she would cure the sick. The Vision replied that she would cure some, but not others, because Our Lord could not depend on them.

Finally, at the end of ten minutes, Lúcia cried, "She is going away now."

The little girl who stood near the Vicar General and had cried out that she saw the luminous globe and then ran down to the green oak, now cried out anew, and, as she pointed with her fingers, exclaimed, "She is going up, she is going up!" and she continued to look and point to the ball of light as it disappeared in the direction of the sun and was absorbed in its light.

The thin, white cloud dissolved, the flowers ceased to fall, and the sun regained its luster. The three children returned to their homes and the crowd dispersed, recounting the wonders they had witnessed.

October 13—

The Day of the Great Miracle

The Heavenly Apparition had repeatedly declared that on October 13 she would disclose her identity and what it was that she desired. In July she had further promised to work a great miracle on that date, as proof of the supernatural origin of the apparitions. Reiterating these promises in September, she added that when she came the following month she would have with her the Infant Jesus and Saint Joseph.

All this had become generally known throughout the land, having been circulated by the many witnesses of the earlier apparitions. The liberal press had derided it, giving irreverent interpretations of the happenings at Fatima. But believers and skeptics alike were intrigued with the "gallant, daring prediction" of a great miracle to take place at a specified date, hour, and place. This was a universal means to test whether or not the apparitions were authentic and divine.

Thus, the whole land waited with keen interest for the great day of October 13. The three little children alone preserved their habitual calm and their sublime simplicity amid the general tension and excitement. On October 11 the Viscount of

Montelo said to Lúcia, "So the Blessed Virgin is going to work a great miracle in order that the whole world will believe that her apparitions are real! Aren't you afraid the people will be angry if the miracle doesn't happen?"

"No," the little girl replied frankly, "I have no fear of that."

On the eve of the great day all paths and roads leading to Fatima were thronged with carriages, bicycles, and crowds on foot. Many walked barefooted. All were saying the rosary or singing hymns as they went along. It was a mobilization of souls desirous of hearing the message brought from heaven, and witnessing the great miracle which, for many, was to confirm their faith. These pilgrims spent the night in the fields, at the very site of the apparitions, to assure themselves of a place near the green oak. No one had any conception as to what the "great miracle" would be, but they had come to wait and see.

Saturday, October 13, 1917, dawned most disappointingly. Contrary to all expectations, daybreak brought rain—steady, cold, and dismal. It seemed as though the Heavenly Visitor were testing the faith and devotion of the pilgrims and giving them a chance to gain merit through a patient acceptance of their discomfort. It then became apparent why the Lady had so emphatically warned the children not to fail to keep the appointment for this day. In such weather they might well have hesitated to go to the hallowed spot, reasonably doubting that the vision would take place under such circumstances. But the bad weather made no difference; the crowd continued to grow. They came from even the most distant towns of the country. Large newspapers sent their representatives and correspondents, and even photographers to record the promised miracle.

The persistent heavy rain had transformed the place into a huge bog. Spectators were without exception drenched to the skin and shivering with cold. At eleven-thirty the crowd was estimated at about 70,000, all having come to see the fulfillment of these four promises:

1. That the Lady would reveal who she was.
2. That she would say what it was she wished and what the message from heaven was which she had come to deliver.
3. That she would be accompanied by the Infant Jesus and Saint Joseph.

4. That she would perform a "great miracle" to testify to the truth of the apparitions and the authenticity of the message.

The children arrived shortly after neatly dressed in their Sunday clothes. Respectfully the crowd made way for them; but, paying no attention to the vast throngs around them, they went directly to the green oak—now reduced by pious spoliation to little more than a skeletal trunk—and stood facing it. Lúcia then called out at the top of her voice, "You must close your umbrellas!" Immediately the people did so, and stood fervently reciting the rosary, unmindful of the pelting rain which soaked through their garments.

The Sixth and Final Apparition

Exactly at midday Lúcia with a slight start stopped praying and cried, "There is the lightning," referring to the flash of light which always heralded the coming of the Lady. Then, looking toward the sky she said, "She is coming!"

"Look well, my child, make sure that you are not deceiving yourself," warned her mother, who had accompanied her and was visibly anxious as to the outcome.

But Lúcia was not deceiving herself; the Lady had come, and the children saw her clearly. As in previous instances, the people were unable to see the apparition, but they saw a white cloud form, like incense, around the children, rise in the air, and gradually disappear.

The procedure of the vision was as before. The Lady dressed in white appeared above the green oak, alone. Lúcia again asked her, "Who are you and what do you want of me?" This is the exact answer as given by the children:

> "She said that she was *Our Lady of the Rosary;* that *we must repent of our sins, change our life, offend Our Lord no more, because He is offended too much; and that we must say our rosary.*"

And the Lady added that she wished a chapel built there in her honor. Then she promised that *"if people would change their lives she would listen to their prayers and the war would quickly end."*

The Great Miracle

The Blessed Virgin when saying goodbye to the children let them understand that this was the last apparition; then suddenly she pointed to the heavens. Raising her head in that direction, Lúcia impulsively cried out, "Oh, look at the sun!"

Of sunlight there had been none that day, and in the pouring rain no one had given a thought to it. Now, however, at the child's cry of wonder, everyone looked up. The 70,000 persons present then began to witness a tremendous and awe-inspiring spectacle which lasted for twelve minutes.

As if by magic the rain suddenly stopped. The clouds broke and scattered wildly, the sky became blue and clear, and the sun shone in the full power of its zenith. But instead of its usual yellow brilliance it was white as a silver disc, so that the people were able to stare at it fixedly without being blinded. Everyone stood looking at what seemed an extraordinary eclipse.

Suddenly *the sun trembled as though shaken by a giant hand, and with a quick, abrupt movement began to spin around like a wheel of fire,* its edges only sparkling. As it gyrated in this way, it projected enormous, multicolored rays of light: green, red, blue, and violet. Like a huge kaleidoscope it colored everything fantastically, the trees, rocks, ground, and the crowd which stood transfixed, with staring eyes watching this overpowering spectacle.

While the people were entranced and lost in this gripping experience, the three children—and they alone—witnessed four successive tableaux which were enacted near the sun.

First, they saw the Holy Family. To the right of the sun was Our Lady of the Rosary in a white gown, but with a blue mantle, instead of the white mantle of all the previous apparitions; to the left was the Infant Jesus and Saint Joseph, both clothed in red.

Second, Our Lord appeared as an adult and lovingly blessed the people.

Third, there appeared Our Lady of the Seven Dolors, the Mater Dolorosa.

Fourth, and last, they saw Our Lady of Mount Carmel holding the scapular in her hand.

After about four minutes the sun ceased its movement as suddenly as it had begun it, but a moment later resumed its fantastic dance, while rays of light and color gave the impression of a gigantic display of fireworks.

Again, at about the end of four minutes, the strange whirling stopped as though to give the spectators respite. But as before, it began again its magical display, appearing ever more varied and colorful. The bystanders thus had ample time to see and consider this impressive, awe-inspiring phenomenon.

During the unforgettable twelve minutes of the miracle the vast crowd stood in suspense, motionless, fascinated, and speechless, not making a sound, seeming hardly to breathe, gazing at the stupendous spectacle which was seen for more than three miles around.

Thus was the great miracle performed on the exact day and at the hour and place designated, to prove the heavenly origin of the apparitions, and to induce the people to obey the message brought by the Blessed Virgin from heaven.

The Culmination of the Miracle

This prolonged and amazing phenomenon had deeply affected those present, filling them with lively sentiments of faith, hope, and adoration; but the most spectacular manifestation of heavenly power was still to come, bringing about genuine conversions and drawing from the people most heartfelt acts of love, contrition, and gratitude.

For the sun, like a gigantic wheel of fire, whose gyrations were rending it apart, seemed suddenly to detach itself from the firmament and to fall straight toward the terrified throng. It appeared to them that now indeed had come the end of the world as foretold in the Gospel when the sun and the stars would fall from the heavens.

From this vast crowd, religiously silent until now, a great cry arose, pregnant with the salutary terror which filled their souls. Acts of contrition were cried aloud by these people convinced that death was at hand, and in utter sincerity preparing themselves by a confession of their sins and a cry for pardon. Some cried, "I believe in God!" others, "Hail Mary, full of grace!" but the greater number called out, "My God, have mercy!" As if inspired by a common impulse they all fell on their knees, unmindful of the rain-soaked ground. Tears and groans filled the air, and loud acts of sorrow for sin were heard, wrung from their very souls.

Just as suddenly the sun stopped its wild careening toward the earth, and its normal color returned as it hung again in a clear sky. And, delicate attention from Mary's maternal heart, whereas all had been drenched to the skin, each was now amazed to find his clothes perfectly dry!

Holy Scripture relates how Moses came down from Mount Sinai, his face radiant from contact with the Divine. So at Fatima: the vast crowd which had just witnessed this sign from heaven, little by little went home, happy, calm, and recollected, fired with love for God and His Blessed Mother. It was like a Pentecostal baptism, a rebirth of faith, confidence, and love in each deeply stirred soul.

Preface
of the
Cardinal Patriarch of Lisbon

Fatima is the work of God. From the very first apparition devotion has grown, miracles have been multiplied, the mysterious event has become known . . . Fatima is not the work of men. It imposes itself against their will. At the outset everything conspired to stifle the glad tidings proclaimed by three innocent children: the hostile unbelief of their families, the prudent reserve of the clergy, the ferocious persecution of the civil authorities.

But within the short span of a quarter of a century the good news of the apparitions of Our Lady at Fatima has gone round the world!

At this time of painful expiation for all mankind, announced by the Blessed Virgin to the little shepherds as a punishment for man's contempt of the Gospel, it is to Our Lady of Fatima that suppliant hands are raised in many quarters of the earth. . . .

It was the compassionate Heart of the Immaculate Virgin which worked the miracle of Fatima. Since that extraordinary event took place a quarter of a century has elapsed, yet the fact remains the same. The finger of God is evident at Fatima.

At first we were of those who paid no attention to the happenings at the Cova da Iria. Pascal remarked that the best cure for credulity is belief: the enlightened Catholic is not an easy believer in miracles. But the evidence presented by the conversions wrought there—a miracle greater by far than the raising of the dead—opened our eyes.

Then we saw . . . what is evident to anyone who wants to open his soul to light: the miraculous character of the apparitions of Fatima.

Everybody knows them. Three children, ingenuous and simple as mountain flowers, declare that the Blessed Virgin appeared to them; their conviction is so clear and so deep that neither force nor blandishments can wrest a denial from their lips; with manly heroism (though crying like children), they walk resolutely to the martyrdom of boiling oil, as they believed in their simplicity, and to die peacefully in the hope that the Lady is coming to take them to paradise.

They announce a great miracle several months before it took place, for a determined day (October 13), so that the people may believe in the reality of the apparitions. The large newspapers publish the extraordinary message in a report meant rather to give the appetizing scandal of the sensational than to give willing testimony to the mysterious action of Providence. On the appointed day, at noon, the rain stopped suddenly, and at the signal of one of the seers who was pointing to the sky, everybody saw a marvelous and astonishing phenomenon in the sun, which scholarly astronomers had not foreseen.

The three little children confess that the Heavenly Apparition had predicted that she would soon come for two of them to take them to heaven. During the illness which struck both they insist that prayers and doctors will never cure them. One of them asserts that she will die alone, far from her family, in a hospital, while the other runs from school to go to church since it is not worth his while to learn how to read. And it all took place as they had predicted. . . .

With the departure of the three little shepherds, pilgrimages to Cova da Iria do not cease. Through the intercession of Mary, Full of Grace, who appeared there, miraculous cures which no human power or human knowledge can produce, take place. One of these was rigorously examined in Rome in the process of canonization of Blessed John de Brito. But, above all, in the Cova da Iria and throughout Portugal, devotion to Our Lady of Fatima brings the grace of conversion which only God can give.

There is no doubt that God has confirmed the truth of the apparition of the Blessed Virgin in the Cova da Iria.

* * *

However, aside from the light shed upon souls, with fruits of penance, little was known of the miracle of Fatima until the publication of *Jacinta*. This book is a new revelation of Fatima. It alone would suffice to clear the doubts that may arise concerning the truth of the apparitions.

The miracle told in this book is the inner miracle of grace, wrought in the souls of the fortunate children to whom it was given to see the Mother of Fair Love. To me this miracle seems the most admirable; it is certainly the most charming. We find in it at the same time the freshness of virginal simplicity and the heights of heroic sanctity. This book cannot be read without the shedding of tears.

After reading it, many will fall upon their knees, if they have not done it before.

This work introduces us into the heart of Fatima. It tells us more about the spirit of Fatima than anything that has as yet been written. If it were not too bold, I would say that it was Our Lady herself who wrote it—in the souls of the seers. Has not St. Paul said that the Christians "were a letter of Christ written not with ink but with the spirit of the living God"? With him we can also say that *Jacinta* is a letter of the Blessed Virgin to be read by souls. It tells us better than words what Our Lady came to do at Fatima, and what she wants of us.

The mystery is now becoming clear. Fatima now speaks not only to Portugal but to the whole world. We believe that the apparitions of Fatima are the beginning of a new epoch, that of the Immaculate Heart of Mary.

What has happened in Portugal proclaims the miracle. It is the presage of what the Immaculate Heart of the Mother of God has prepared for the world.

† MANUEL CARDINAL GONÇALVES CEREJEIRA
Patriarch of Lisbon

Fifty Years Ago

Mountain life at Fatima fifty years ago! What fond memories of a time which will never return! The roads are few, and no one disturbs the peaceful lives of the good mountain people. Down stony trails they go on holidays to the fiesta and on market day to the surrounding villages where they sell their produce and buy the necessities of life for the family. Their purchases are few: a gold necklace, earrings, a few earthenware pots, kitchenware, a little hat for the girl, a belt for the boy. As to the rest, the family is self-subsistent. From time to time they buy farm tools; the well-to-do buy a pair of bullocks, or see to the mending of the donkey's saddle or crupper. They go to the village to pay the tithes.

These are the only trips they make. The fact is that a trip is not pleasant. "Going down, all the saints help you," the proverb goes, but it is hardly so in this case. The hills are steep, and the descent dangerous for the poor animals; the riders themselves have to be very careful lest the donkey throw its burden.

There are two trails: one follows the mountain ridge down to the plain; the other leads down to the outskirts of Moinhos. At the top, the latter cuts across a narrow valley toward Fonte Nova, and reaches to Alvega; it passes the chapel of Saint Sebastian and Melroeira on its way to the village. This is the better road. But it is frightening to take it, for it suddenly dips between two steep mountains which soar on both sides, scarred here and there by straggling woods or hardy shrubs which alone can take root in the parched fissures of the rocks. No matter how you strain your eyes, there is not a soul in sight. One could kill and flay a poor traveler, and his groans would reach no human heart.

At the foot of the mountain the prospect seems even more frightening, for there is a sudden opening in the rock from which gushes forth a flood of fresh water, the only fountain in the whole village. It is the Fonte Nova.

Yet not even this oasis brightens the solitary way by which the people descend from the mountain to the village. It reminds one of the wild abode of the anchorites spoken of in the lives of the saints of old. The climb home is not easier, for the donkeys are not accustomed to such efforts in the short space of a day. All these circumstances force the mountain people to lead a home life.

The land, thanks be to God, gives them everything. In the cracks of the rocks grow, as if by miracle, green and sturdy fruit trees. God be praised! The land, when cleared of stones, provides rich cereal, maize, and garden produce. From below, the mountain appears bare and stony to the casual observer, yet from above it is seen to be a garden walled with loose stones. In spring the almond tree, the peach and apple, the plum and cherry, flower into soft banks of delicate whiteness; in summer and fall they heap the table, delight the children, and fatten the cattle.

Countless flocks dot the mountains and valleys. From them the people of the mountain obtain all they need: fertilizer for the land, plenty of milk and cheese, meat from the lambs, and from the sheep wool for their rough stockings and cloaks. They are almost independent. Their life is sober and frugal—they have good bread, good oil in stone containers, potatoes and other vegetables, pork from the hogs they raise on the acorns. The result is excellent health and long lives.

The small homes are easily heated. The windows are narrow and low, for in the mountain no one lacks sun and air. In the kitchen there is an old table, a tripod of oak for the fire place, a dozen plates and bowls of white crockery from Coimbra, two or three yellow pots and kettles of glassy clay, but little else. In some places not even this much is found, for the family still eats in common from a small earthen pan around which they gather, just as they join together during the day for the common work.

In the parlor there is a rustic table, on which stands the crucifix. Above it, on the wall, there is a multitude of holy pictures—for this reason the room is often called "The Saints' House" (*casa dos santinhos*). Two large pine chests and two chairs complete the furnishings. The beds are made up of benches, usually with plenty of clothes. They are covered with a blanket, made with shreds of cloth, or with a woolen quilt woven on the family loom.

Beside the house is the fold in which the sheep are kept at night. The garden and the fields about are dominated by fig trees, under the shade of which the mountain people enjoy the long summer afternoons when the heat is intense. In the rocks are dug wells and cisterns, from which it is a real pleasure to drink the cool and refreshing water that gushes forth. There is little wine to be had, and the people purchase little.

The men, working on the farm or in the mountain forests, lead a crude and laborious life. They wear sandals and rough clothes. The children shepherd the sheep and few of them learn to read. As they advance in age they leave the flocks to take on work according to their sex and condition. The family is the great school for them. Man or woman, each must know how to make a living. The woman stays at home to cook, spin, weave, clean the house, wash the clothes, and to care for her children or for her brothers.

The mountain woman is tender and charming. It may be said that the old Moorish customs are still prevalent there, but that is not entirely true. It is only the flowering of the Christian life which gives the woman her proper place as queen of the home.

Sunday is the day of the Lord and the day of rest. In the morning everybody goes to Mass.

Only the very old and the sick, or the mothers
with infant children, stay at home. If there are two
Masses, they take turns. The village presents an air
of festivity and joy. People put on their Sunday
best; the men wear a peculiar hood-like cap, a short
coat with clasps allowing the shirt to be seen in the
back above the trousers. These latter are held by a
belt and are open above the shoetop in the shape
of a bell. The men folk also carry in their hands a
crook of quince or oak. In winter the women wear
over their backs a large cloaklike skirt which pro-
tects them from curious eyes and from the cutting
breath of the north wind. In the summer time they
wear a graceful little hat at the rim of which are
tied two tips of the kerchief, folded in three parts,
while the third tip drops down over the neck and
shoulders. Bright colors are popular among the
young women folk: cream, yellow, pink, and flesh
color. They wear a large blouse which is bound to
the skirt of baize by a wide band of red cloth. Their
hair is meticulously parted in the middle.

Mass is over. A few words to their friends
and a brief commentary on the day's sermon.
Now and then a baptism may draw the attention of the women, curious about the baby and
its layette. An hour later the church is deserted

and so it remains throughout the day, unless at dusk the more devout and the youth of courting age come to prayers at the call of the parish priest during certain seasons of the year. The remainder of the day is devoted to rest, to the family, and to friends. They eat breakfast leisurely, since work does not press as during the week; in the summer they take their siesta and spend the afternoon under the shade of the trees which surround the house. There they sit and talk. There are no newspapers, or leaflets, but the older folks and those endowed with a lively imagination tell to spellbound children the adventures of the brigands who infest various parts of the country. The African campaigns, the Liberal Wars which in the neighboring village of Ourém caused much suffering and misery, and even the French invasion of the early nineteenth century, are topics of interest, told with many a true episode and, unconsciously, a great many more which are fictitious.

In the Shadow
of the Cross

The road divides as it nears the churchyard, coming from Cova da Iria across Fatima, toward Vila Nova de Ourém. To the right it leads southward to Montelo and Casa Velha. Narrow and deserted, it is called the Montelo road. A few feet down this road, on the right, there is a wide gate of wrought iron, and above it, on the masonry this simple and truthful inscription:

Nós ossos que aqui estamos
Pelos vossos esperamos.

We bones here at rest await
Your own to pass beneath this gate.

This is the entrance to the cemetery of Fatima. From here easily discernible at the left is a tomb which rises above the others. It is very simple, all white, and built of the stone which abounds in the land. In spite of its complete simplicity, however, it is the most remarkable of all.

Far away, the bald and arid tops of the Serra d'Aire block the horizon in broken but clear outline. At closer range are other mountains and scattered hamlets, and in our immediate vicinity there are houses and fields where life goes on normally. On the other side of the little road are the churchyard, the parish church, and the rectory.

There is a path, paved with stones, through the middle of the narrow cemetery. Here and there rises a tombstone and near us shoots up the shattered trunk of an old cypress tree which the years have left sad and lonely at the gate, as if to protect the white sepulcher at its feet; but now that the cyclone has passed by, it remains only a symbol of the life that was. The tomb is that of Francisco and Jacinta Marto, the little shepherds who saw the Vision in the Cova da Iria. Let us kneel and pray, for holy is the ground we tread. A brief inscription tells us:

Here lie the mortal remains
of Francisco and Jacinta
To whom Our Lady appeared.

D. José Alves Correia da Silva, Bishop of the diocese of Leiria, ordered the erection of this tomb and the transfer thereto of the remains of Jacinta which, since February 24, 1920, had been resting in a lead casket in the family sepulcher of the Barons of Alvaiázere, in the cemetery of Vila Nova de Ourém. The remains of Francisco, which had lain there since the day of his burial, were also removed to Fatima, September 12, 1935. We were not privileged to assist at the ceremony, but from trustworthy witnesses we have heard the story of all that took place, from Vila Nova de Ourém until the final sealing of the casket in the new abode which the loving hands of the venerable Bishop had constructed in front of the church where the little shepherds had been baptized.

After all the necessary preparations in the cemetery of Vila Nova de Ourém, the casket was opened and all the spectators were struck with amazement as they beheld the face of Jacinta perfectly preserved. Miracle? Natural phenomenon? Let the experts give the answer. What is certain is that Jacinta died a victim of a purulent pleurisy; moreover, the usual amount of lime was thrown upon her body. It was not expected, therefore, that under such circumstances the body should escape corruption. Was the rest of it in the same condition? The haste with which everything was done precluded further investigation. Several persons touched the remains of Jacinta with handkerchiefs and religious articles. After the casket was closed, the funeral procession headed for Fatima.

The Barons of Alvaiázere were reluctant to let go from their sepulcher a jewel they considered almost their own. In a letter to the Bishop of Leiria the present Baron wrote the following: "It was with eyes filled with tears that we saw leave our tomb the relic which obtained for me and for mine so many evident graces from Heaven. . . ." There were only four cars in the funeral procession. The Baron and his son carried the urn containing the remains of Jacinta. There were two priests in surplice and stole, the Reverend Doctors João Pereira Venancio and Luis Fischer, the parents of the seer, and a few ladies. When everything was in order, the cortege proceeded through Vila Nova de Ourém where formerly the Jacobin fury had struggled in vain to wrest the secret from her heart.

As they climbed the road, they left to one side and above, to the east, the old castle of Vila Nova de Ourém, noble in the blood of its family and traditions as well as in the sad grandeur of its ruins. The heat was oppressive. Now and then we heard the lonely song of far-off birds. From the roadside and the open fields came the monotonous chirping of numberless crickets. The fertile lands around, the vineyards, the crops, the gardens, and all the life in them, were unaware of the simple and solemn procession which at the hour of siesta was heading toward Fatima.

The climb was long, but now the village lay far below, and the castle seemed level with their feet. On both sides, between deep and precipitous ravines, rises the mountain chain. On the right, windmills watch like village sentinels. On the left, the view sweeps over mountains and hills which crowd one upon another until they are lost in a vague shimmering, blending earth and sky. The cortege reached Fatima at high noon, sun time. Followed by many priests and faithful, they entered the holy place of the apparitions. The Archbishop of Evora said Mass in the chapel of confessions and presided at the remainder of the funeral service.

Gradually, as the news was spread abroad, pilgrims came to touch the urn with religious articles which they devoutly kept as souvenirs.

At the end of the services everybody returned to the cemetery to lay to rest, with flowers and prayers, the bodies of the two little shepherds whom the Blessed Virgin had united in the inestimable grace of the apparitions. Christian piety reunited them in the rest of their earthly remains, while their souls, we trust, enjoy the delights, love, and everlasting vision of the Beautiful Lady, the beloved Heavenly Mother.

CHAPTER

3

The Flower Blooms

Senhora Olimpia de Jesus was the widow of José Fernandes Rosa. On February 17, 1897, she entered upon a second marriage with Manuel Marto, who was then twenty-four years of age. No one could tell Senhora Olimpia was four years older than her second husband. They decided to live in the house which had been built for Senhora Olimpia's first marriage. Their large room faced the door of the parlor. In this room was born to them, on February 1, 1899, the first of nine children. Here also, like all her brothers and half-brothers, was born Jacinta, the youngest of the family, on March 11, 1910. Her parents welcomed her with joy, for at that time the perverse notion that children are a burden to their parents had not yet become general. Children were regarded rather as a blessing from God. This eleventh child[2] was to prove more than an ordinary blessing.

Large families are generally wholesome. The parents manifest a profound spirit of faith and sacrifice and a true understanding of the high mission entrusted to them by the Creator. The children grow up in the love of work and even of suffering. The grace of God pervades the gladsome atmosphere of the home. From these families, ordinarily the best, come the finest and most beautiful characters. The curse of God falls heavily upon the homes which voluntarily suppress life or limit it with revolting cynicism and selfishness, thus robbing God and country of the children owed to both.

Because she was the youngest, Jacinta was covered with caresses by the entire family. At night, after work, and on Sunday afternoon, the little child lived a difficult life, from lap to lap; everybody wanted to hold her. She was kissed and squeezed and dragged about everywhere. At times it was necessary for Senhora Olimpia to pretend that she was utterly displeased with all the fuss made over her child, but her mother's heart rejoiced that so

2 Senhora Olimpia had two children by her first husband.

much love was lavished upon her youngest daughter. Mothers are like that. Jacinta spent most of her time at home in the midst of this love and devotion. Her older sisters tended the flocks. From her mother's lips Jacinta learned her catechism and her prayers. She yearned for the day when, dressed all in white like an angel, she would receive her Lord in the Blessed Sacrament for the first time.

Some may find it strange that in writing the life of Jacinta I do not present her as a prodigy of holiness come down from heaven for our delight and edification. But we must portray her as she really was, as far as we know, with her virtues and her faults as they come before us.

We want to introduce our readers to the true Jacinta, the real little girl to whom Our Lord granted only a very brief sojourn in this world. A saint is not something which drops from heaven, already made with an unchangeable disposition; a saint is rather the happy outcome of the intimate cooperation of man with the grace of God. Saints are not born saints; God makes them such if they will it. Holiness, moreover, is not something foreign to our life and times. To it are called all Christians of every time and in every place. "Be ye perfect," said the Master to His followers, and His voice echoes throughout the centuries and awakens in souls the thirst for perfection. Let no one think that holiness is the absence of every imperfection. Holiness consists in love, in charity. Imperfections are to holiness what rust is to iron: if fire heats iron, the rust is consumed and the iron is made brilliant and luminous. Such is the action of love on the soul of the saints.

We must speak now of the "rust" in Jacinta's life. The faults and imperfections which we note in her life are evident proof of the transformation later effected in her soul by grace, and of the generosity with which she responded to the workings of the Holy Spirit. If there is anything which can move and edify, it is the example of little children who heroically give their blood and life in witness to their faith and their love of the Divine Master, Our Lord Jesus Christ. The words of Saint Augustine, "So small in age, yet so big in sin," can be changed for the glory of God to read, "So small in age, yet so big in love." Though only children, they are like budding blossoms which fill the air with fragrance. It is the "good odor of Christ" which from them is scattered all over the world. Blessed be God, Who in our time has raised so great and admirable a flowering of holiness among little children.

Before the apparition, Jacinta was an ordinary child. She was attractive and strong and also the victim of the defects common among children. Lúcia,[3] her cousin, and the oldest of the three who saw the apparitions, has written on this point:

"Before the events of 1917, with the exception of the bond of relationship which united us, no other particular affection urged me to prefer the companionship of Jacinta to that of Francisco or of any other child. On the contrary, her company was at times really undesirable because of her very sensitive temperament. The least quarrel which arose among the children during the games was enough to send her pouting to a corner. No amount of caressing and coaxing could move her to return to the game. It was necessary to let her choose the game and the partner she wanted.

"But even then, she had a good heart and God had endowed her with a sweet and loving character which made her at once amiable and attractive. Both Jacinta and her little brother Francisco had a special liking for me and nearly always asked me to play with them. They did not enjoy the company of the other children, and so we had our games near

3 Lúcia is now a Sister of Saint Dorothy, at Tuy, Spain. See Chapter 24.

the well which belonged to my parents. Once we arrived there Jacinta chose the games. She preferred to play with little pebbles and buttons, sitting on the stones of the well, under the plum trees. Not infrequently I found myself in great distress, for when I was called for meals I noticed that all my buttons were gone. Ordinarily she had won them from me, and that was enough to prompt a scolding from my mother. It was necessary to sew them on hurriedly, but it was difficult to get them back from her, because besides being very sensitive she was also very grasping. She wanted to keep them for the next game and so save her own. It was only under the threat that I would never play with her again that she relented and gave them back to me."

Besides having the inclination to pout and to be acquisitive, faults she later learned to overcome, Jacinta was very fond of dancing. "We were so very fond of dancing," writes Lúcia, "that whenever any of the shepherds played an instrument we immediately began to dance. Jacinta, even though she was so small, had a special aptitude for it." So great was their passion for dancing and playing that while the flocks were grazing over the hills they made only a pretense of saying the rosary, thus to be free and left to themselves.

Lúcia relates: "We had been told to say the rosary after lunch but we wanted every minute for play and so we came upon a fine way of going through it in a hurry: we ran the beads through our fingers and on each one merely said 'Hail Mary,' 'Hail Mary'; when we came to the end of the decade we pronounced very slowly the words of the Our Father. And so we had said our rosary in the twinkling of an eye."

It is not surprising that the children were born with a taste for dancing. It was the general inclination of that time, especially after the war. Hence there developed the necessity to fight stubbornly and methodically against an entertainment which led to corruption so many innocent souls who found in it incentives to sin. Lúcia tells what happened in this regard when she was ten years old. The parish priest at the time of the apparitions, Father Manuel Marques Ferreira, had replaced Father Pena, who had died. It was Father Ferreira who energetically started the campaign against dancing.

From Lúcia's pen we read: "When he [Father Ferreira] learned about the pagan custom of dancing which prevailed in the parish, he immediately began to preach against it from the pulpit. In public and in private he took every opportunity to combat this evil custom. As soon as my mother heard the parish priest, she forbade my sisters to go to any entertainment of that kind, and since the example of my sisters dissuaded others from going, the custom gradually disappeared from our parish. The same thing happened with the children who formed their own dancing groups. One day someone told my mother:

"'Up to now it was not a sin to dance, but now because the new priest has arrived has it become a sin? How is that?'

"My mother answered:

"'I do not know; what I know is that the parish priest does not want dancing and so my daughters will not return to those entertainments; the most I will do will be to let them dance a little within the family; the priest says family dancing is not a sin.'"

4

Signs
of Greatness

A t the break of day the sunflower seeks the
sun, to live in the charm of its contemplation. When plants spring up away from
light they grow and stretch out to reach it, for
light is the secret of their life. Such was Jacinta.
From infancy her whole life was a climbing toward
the light, a striving which filled and possessed her
being. Like every normal child Jacinta loved to
play. But even in her games and diversions she
consciously endeavored never to offend Our Lord.
The thought of God never left her. She felt a holy
curiosity about God and the things of God. She
wept sincerely over the pains and sorrows of Our
Lord. She was endowed with an angelic sensibility
of love for Jesus and with an ardent yearning to

contemplate Him. Such were the earliest manifestations of this chosen soul. How many great lessons are embodied here for the children of today and, above all, for educators and for those who form the souls of children and of youth! The soul of a child is indifferent to nothing. Games, stories, feasts, conversations, and friendships exercise a decisive influence in the souls of the little ones.

Sister Maria Lúcia said that she owes the preservation of her innocence partly to the company of Jacinta. With much greater reason today, parents and educators should take special care to choose suitable surroundings in which the Divine Gardener may help them to rear and nourish the tender plants entrusted to their care. On this point Sister Maria Lúcia writes well in telling us of the first steps in the life of her innocent cousin:

"One of her favorite games was that of *forfeit*, a game in which the winner commands the loser to do whatever he wants him to do. She loved to send us after butterflies for her. At other times she would ask for some flower of her liking. One day as we were playing this game in the house of my parents, my turn came to command her. My brother was writing near the table. I told her to kiss him.

"'Not that,' she cried, 'tell me to do something else. Why don't you tell me to kiss that crucifix over there?' It was the crucifix hanging on the wall."

"'All right,' I answered, 'climb that chair, bring the crucifix over here, kneel down, and kiss and embrace it three times, once for Francisco, once for me, and once for yourself.'

"She answered: 'I will kiss Our Lord as many times as you want.' Running for the crucifix, she kissed it with a devotion I have never forgotten. Then looking attentively at Our Lord, she asked: 'Why is Our Lord nailed like that to the cross?'"

"'Because He died for us,' I answered.

"'Tell me all about it, please.'

"In the evening my mother used to tell us stories. Together with fairy tales and the stories of golden princesses and royal pigeons, which father and mother and my older sisters would tell us, my mother would relate the story of the Passion, of St. John the Baptist, etc. I knew, therefore, the Passion of Our Lord like a story, and since it was enough for me to hear stories once to repeat them in detail, I began point by point to tell my friends the history of the life of Our Lord.

"When my sister passed near, noticing that we had the crucifix, she took it from us and reprimanded me, saying that I must not touch such holy things. Jacinta got up, ran for my sister, and said: 'Mary, don't scold her. I did it, but I won't do it again.' My sister caressed her, bidding us to go out to play, because in the house we would leave nothing in its proper place.

"We left for the well, which was located at the bottom of the garden, to continue our story. We chose this spot because it was hidden behind several chestnut trees, a heap of stones, and a wall of shrubbery. Several years later we were to choose this very place as the cell of our colloquies, of our fervent prayers, and as the witness of our bitter tears. Jacinta wept as she heard the story of the sufferings of Our Lord. Many times afterward she would ask me to repeat it. Then, crying with grief, she would say: 'O poor Jesus! I will never do any sin. I don't want Jesus to suffer any more.'

"During siesta, and that especially in the Lenten season, my mother taught her children the catechism. At one time Jacinta, too, was there. One of the children accused another of having said ugly words. My mother reprimanded both with all severity. She told them that ugly words are not to be said, that it was a sin to say them, and that the Child Jesus was displeased and would send to hell sinners who did not go to confession. Jacinta did not forget the lesson. On the first day that she came to the children's meeting she asked me: 'Won't your mother let you go today?'

"'No,' I replied.

"'Then I am going to my backyard with Francisco,' she said.

"'Why don't you stay here?' I asked.

"'My mother does not want us to stay here with these other people; she told us to play in our backyard—she does not want us to learn those sinful things which the Child Jesus does not like.'

"Then she whispered in my ear: 'If your mother lets you go, will you come to my house?'

"'Yes,' I answered.

"'Then go ask her,' she suggested. And taking her brother's hand, she went home.

"My sister belonged to the Sodality of the Sacred Heart. Each time she went to Communion she took me along to receive. On one occasion my aunt took her little daughter to see the ceremony. Jacinta fixed her eyes on the 'angels' who strewed flowers before the Blessed Sacrament. From that day on she would now and then go away from the group when we were playing, to gather a bunch of flowers which she threw at me one by one.

"'Jacinta, why on earth are you doing a thing like that?' I asked.

"'Because the angels did it; I am only throwing flowers at you.'

"It was my sister's wont to dress a few little girls in angel costumes for the Feast of Corpus Christi. Their task was to strew flowers in the procession of the Blessed Sacrament. I was always one of the chosen girls. One day I told Jacinta about the coming feast, and she asked me to plead with my sister to let her go with me. We went together to ask this favor. My sister consented. She tried a costume on Jacinta, and in the rehearsals carefully told us how to strew flowers for the Child Jesus.

"'Do we see Him?' asked Jacinta with great interest.

"'Yes,' my sister answered, 'the pastor carries Him.'

"Jacinta was very happy and continually asked if the feast was still too far away. Finally the longed-for day arrived, and Jacinta was beside herself with joy. We took our place first by the altar, and later in the procession, each of us carrying a basket of flowers. I strewed mine on the places designated by my sister, but it was impossible to draw Jacinta's attention to her flowers—she did not strew a single one. She just looked at Father Ferreira, and nothing more.

"When the ceremony was over my sister led us out of the church and asked Jacinta, 'Why didn't you strew the flowers in front of Jesus?'

"'Because I did not see Him,' Jacinta answered, and then asked me, 'Did you see the Child Jesus?'

"'No, but don't you know that we cannot see the Child Jesus in the Host? He is hidden. He is the one we receive in Communion.'

"'Do you talk with Him when you receive Communion?'

"'I do.'

"'Why don't you see Him?'

"'Because He is hidden.'

"'I am going to ask my mother to let me go to Communion.'

"'But the pastor will not give you Communion before you are ten years old.'

"'You are not ten yet, but you have received Communion. . . .'

"'That is because I knew all the catechism, and you don't know it yet.'

"After this they asked me to teach the catechism; so I became the catechist for my two companions, who learned with extraordinary enthusiasm. But though I could answer all the questions when they were put to me, I could remember only a few points here and there to teach them.

"This led Jacinta to say to me one day, 'Teach us something else. We know that already.'

"I confessed that I could not remember the subjects unless I was questioned, and I added, 'Ask your mother to let you go to the church and learn.'

"Since they wanted to receive the Hidden Jesus, as they called Him, they placed the request before their mother. My aunt consented, but did not allow them to go very frequently, because the church was far away and they were too small. Besides, the pastor would not give them Communion before they were ten. Jacinta was always questioning me about the Hidden Jesus.

"One day she asked me: 'How is it that so many people receive the Hidden Jesus at the same time? Is there a little piece for each one?'

"'Don't you see that there are many Hosts, and that the Child Jesus is in each one of them? . . .'"

CHAPTER 5

Child Love

One of the most charming aspects of little Jacinta's life is the deep friendship which bound her to her cousin Lúcia, and the fidelity with which she preserved it throughout life. Childhood play and ties of blood gave rise to it, and the enthusiasm with which they took their first steps to the tabernacle confirmed it. A common vocation to great things, which they later testified, consecrated it; and their life of piety and mortification intensified it. As long as they are unable to rebind it in heaven together, the fond memory of the chalice of suffering from which they drank abundantly is its final crown.

They could not live apart from each other. Evidence of this is given by Lúcia in the following facts: they always played together, and the day on which they could not was not a happy one for either. Jacinta was always inviting Lúcia to play with her, but the request could not always be complied with. Lúcia herself tells about it:

"Frequently I was unable to satisfy the desire of my little cousin friend. Since my older sisters lived at home—the one a weaver and the other a seamstress—the neighbors usually asked my mother to let their children play in our backyard, near me and under the vigilance of my sisters, while the neighbors themselves went to work in the fields. My mother never refused, although it entailed a loss of time for my sisters. I was in charge of those children, and had to see to it that they did not fall into the well in our yard. We were shaded there from the sun by three large fig trees, whose branches we used for swings. There was also an old threshing-floor that served for a dining-room. On those days when Jacinta would come for me to go to our usual retreat at the well I said that I could not go because my mother had told me to stay where I was."

At such times the two of them would resign themselves sorrowfully to their fate and take part in the games. But the worst was yet to come. Lúcia was a little woman now, and could not be at play all the time. She was going to become a shepherdess. This is how she tells it:

"In the meantime I had reached the age at which my mother was accustomed to send her children to keep the flocks. My sister Carolina was now thirteen and had to find work. So my mother placed me in charge of our sheep. I broke the news to my companions and told them that I could no longer play with them. They could not reconcile themselves to the separation, and so they asked their mother to let them go with me, but she refused. We had to resign ourselves. So almost every evening they would wait for me on the road, and then for a while we would play in the yard, until Our Lady and the Angels lit the tiny candles of the sky and put them in the window to illumine us, as we would say.

"The little ones could scarcely get along without their cousin. For that reason they constantly begged their mother to let them also keep their sheep. My aunt, perhaps to rid herself of their importunity, allowed them at last to tend the sheep, even though they were too small. Beaming with happiness, they came to tell me the news, and to plan the way in which we would gather the sheep every day. Each would take out his little flock at the appointed hour, but the first one would wait for the others on the *Barreiro,* a small pond at the foot of the mountain. Once we were together we would decide on the pasture for that day, and rush over to it as happy and joyful as if going to a feast."

It seemed, however, that Our Lord wanted to test the firmness of that friendship and purify it well through suffering. Who would have said at first sight that their new life alone on the mountain and in the valley would ever be disturbed? Yet this was one of the results of the apparitions. People were always coming to talk to them. It was necessary to search all over for them, and to find someone to take their place minding the sheep. This was very troublesome for their parents, brothers, and sisters, as well as a true martyrdom for the children themselves, who, as we shall see later, found one of their heaviest crosses in those visits and interviews. It could not go on like this. Sister Lúcia writes:

"My aunt grew tired of sending for her children so frequently, and so she put João in charge of the flocks. Jacinta took the change very hard for two reasons: she had to speak to everyone who came around and, as she put it, she could not be with me all day long. For the time being my mother thought it sufficient to assign me to a definite field, so that she would know where I was when needed. When the field happened to be nearby, I would inform my companions, who would come to me as soon as they could. Jacinta would run until she got near me. Then tired from running, she would sit down and call for me, and would not keep quiet until I answered and ran toward her. At long last, however, my mother grew tired of seeing my sister waste time in going for me and taking my place with the flock, so she decided to sell it. In agreement with my aunt, my two companions and I were sent to school."

The fruit was almost ripe. Soon the Lord would come to reap it. The last and greatest tribulation and the strongest proof of that now perfectly supernaturalized friendship were at hand. Jacinta fell ill, and had to be hospitalized. It was the final separation. The tenderness which she had manifested throughout her life was intensified. She foresaw the end, and the idea of separation caused her added suffering. Lúcia never left her mind. Jacinta's heart bled with sorrow. Even when Our Lady visited her in bed, in the heavenly conversation she did not forget her cousin. Later she told Lúcia:

"I asked her if you were going with me. She answered, 'no.' This is what grieved me most. She told me that my mother was taking me over there, and that afterward I would be left alone."

Then, after remaining thoughtful for a moment, she added, "If you could only come with me! What pains me most is to go without you. I am afraid the hospital is a very dark house where no one can see anything, and I am going to suffer there all alone!"

Lúcia narrates: "The day arrived on which she was to go to the hospital, where she had much to suffer. When her mother visited her at Vila Nova de Ourém, she asked Jacinta if she wanted anything. She said that she wanted to see me. As soon as she could, my aunt, at the cost of innumerable sacrifices, took me along. When Jacinta saw me, she joyfully hugged me, and asked her mother to leave me with her and go out to do her shopping. The time for my visit passed by rapidly, and my aunt returned to take me back. Again she asked Jacinta if she wanted anything, but Jacinta asked her only to bring me again when she returned to see her. My good aunt, who wanted to please her little daughter, took me there a second time."

Jacinta was very deeply impressed with the idea of dying alone. Solitude and isolation frightened her as she saw this sorrow approaching. Lúcia consoled her, urging her to be tranquil because Our Lady was coming for her.

Jacinta answered: "I don't know why it is, but at times I don't remember that she is coming for me. I only remember that I am to die without you near me!"

"Finally the day of departure for Lisbon arrived," writes Sr. Lúcia. "The parting was very moving. She embraced me for a long time, and weeping she said, 'We will never see each other again. Pray hard for me, until I go to heaven. Then I'll ask very much for you there. Never tell the secret to anyone even if they kill you. Love Jesus very much, and also the Immaculate Heart of Mary, and make many sacrifices for sinners.'

"From Lisbon she sent me word that Our Lady had been there to see her, and that she had revealed to her the hour and the day on which she was to die. She urged me again to be very good."

Jacinta was tender, simple, and innocent like the lambs with which she played. This was a family trait or, still more, a personal gift with which Our Lord had enriched her, and which she had perfected in her life of shepherdess. One day she revealed, contrary to their agreement, that she had seen the Blessed Mother. Lúcia reprimanded her twice, and twice Jacinta expressed sorrow for having caused trouble, and cried, asking for forgiveness. "The poor child, as she heard my reasons, began to cry," writes Sister Maria Lúcia, "and, as previously in May, she asked me for forgiveness."

Jacinta's friendship for Lúcia will remain one of the most beautiful testimonies to the beauty of her heart. Later, after the apparitions, she will manifest the same sensitive and affectionate kindness in the sadness and retirement brought on by a realization of the offenses against Our Lord and, on a more natural plane, in the immense longing she felt for her little brother Francisco, whom pneumonia had taken away, but whom she did not forget even in her own illness. Sister Maria Lúcia in a few words has depicted Jacinta's sorrow:

"She suffered a great deal because of her brother's illness. For a long time she would remain in a thoughtful mood and if anyone asked her what she was thinking of, she would answer, 'Francisco. I wish I could see him!' And her eyes would fill with tears.

"One day I said to her, 'It won't be long now before you go to heaven, but in my case. . . .'

"'Don't cry,' she responded. 'I will pray for you very much up there. It is Our Lady who wants it thus.'"

Such was Jacinta. Sensitive, humble, tender, and friendly. These same traits, with slight difference, were those of the Jacinta of the apparitions. Would that today's friendships were like this—firm, wholesome, deeply Christian, and supernatural!

Mountain Beauty

The ability to feel the beauty of things and thus to rise to God is one of the most impressive characteristics of the seers of Fatima. There are many erroneous judgments made about the three little shepherds because of a photograph we have of them. Their dress, their looks, and features all urge us to look upon them as somewhat boorish and almost semi-savage. However, behind that exterior are hidden souls and hearts charged with an extraordinary sensibility. We have already seen this in the chapter on their friendship. Now we shall see how they saw, felt, and loved the beauty which God scattered through the world for our delight and enjoyment. Without expecting it, we shall encounter souls of artists, souls of poets. But this will not surprise us if we remember that most saints are poets at heart.

Look at an Augustine, a Francis of Assisi, an Ignatius of Loyola, a Therese of the Child Jesus, an Anthony of Lisbon. In each you are aware of a soul endowed with the power of feeling deeply and of penetrating beneath the exterior of earthly things. One might say that their souls vibrate under the touch of beauty that is the image and participation of uncreated Beauty. Francis of Assisi went through the forest, talked with birds, sang to the sun, to the water, to the snow, and to everything that was beautiful. Augustine spent numberless hours in contemplating the immense beauty of the sea. Ignatius of Loyola turned to the little flowers of the field, for their very beauty is a hymn of praise to the God who made them. Filled with their song, Ignatius told them to be silent, for he was well aware of their invitation to praise Him, too. Likewise many other saints, moved by the frequent contemplation of the boundless beauty of God, easily perceived the immense harmony of the universe, from the most grandiose spectacles to the smallest things.

How many beautiful scenes the Lord has sown on the mountains! What a wealth of contemplation for those who live there! The rising and setting of the sun, the limpid and starry sky, nights washed by moonlight, broad horizons seen from the top of the cliffs, flower banks clothing the mountain land in the spring, the singing and simple amusements of pastoral life—all these afford many occasions for the soul to contemplate created beauty. From this it is but a step to rise to God.

Sister Maria Lúcia reveals this in the following words: "Little Jacinta loved to go at dusk to the yard in front of our house. Here she would drink in the beauty of the setting sun and of the starlit sky . . . she was enraptured by moonlight nights . . . there we vied with each other to see who could count more stars."

What beautiful sunsets the mountains at Fatima present! The chain of dells and hills, here clothed in luxuriant vegetation, there white and bald with their walls and cliffs, and on the heights the tireless wind-mills—all these enrich the landscape with such a variety of color that the setting sun becomes a spectacle of fascinating beauty.

More to the left can be seen the outline of Serra d'Aire which the clear atmosphere brings so close to us that they seem no more than a gunshot away. There is no dust on the mountains; the north wind or the sea breeze sweeps them clean. Hence the eye can travel far into the distance.

The sun has sunk beyond the mountain which rises on the other side of the Eira da Pedra and Casa Velha, but still on the Cabeço, on the surrounding heights, on the church steeple, on the windmills of Fatima, on the broken line of Serra d'Aire, all is gold, poured out with infinite prodigality: golden houses, golden cliffs, golden trees. And when the mists of evening fall, even the air is golden bright. While the eyes are caught in so great a beauty, the imagination calls forth tales of fairies, princesses, and charmed Moorish maidens in the midst of fabulous treasures surrounded by the mists of mystery.

In such a rapture is spent the nostalgic hour in which day enters into agony and dies, and the soul is filled with deep longing and ineffable sadness. It grieves and dies with the sad things which life abandons. . . . The frogs croak in the lakes and swamps. Hidden away in the thick of the grass, the crickets join the song. Toads and snakes partake of the great feast of the end of day, and the locusts swell the chorus with their monotonous chirping.

The sound of little bells announces the return of the sheep from pasture. The mothers call for the little lambs strayed on the way, and the shepherd with his whistle announces the arrival at the fold where, calling them by name and lightly tapping them with a stick, he separates his own from the other sheep. The strange glow of fireflies pricks the air. And when, aroused from the sweet repose induced by the solemn night prayer which arises from earth to the Creator, the spell is broken and the children raise their eyes, already the shades of night cover with mystery the life of the earth, and a veil of darkness envelops them on every side.

On clear nights one can look from the heights and see the mountain illumined by the sheen of the soft light of the moon gently poured out upon all the contours of the earth. The whitened stones look like pale shadows of things from another world. In a limpid and deep sky myriads of stars draw the gaze of the little spectators. Unwittingly the three friends are struck with the same thought that filled the minds of the Fathers of the Church, who in their day looked at the moon and called it Lamp of Our Lady; looked at the stars and called them Lamps of the Angels.

Flowers played an important role in the life
and affections of Jacinta. If it is true, as the Ital-
ians say, that we become gentle in the presence of
flowers, the predilection which Jacinta showed for
them gives us a deeper understanding of how her
brief and simple life can be a source of inspiration
for the children of today. The mountain has no
gardens, but by the side of the houses, rustic and
simple, there is always a flower-bed, a little corner
where the water left from household chores makes
the very stones bloom.

The mountain has no gardens nor does it
need them, since it is, for the greater part of the
year, an immense garden which the prodigal hand
of the Creator cultivates and preserves with the
loving care of the busy gardener. Lilies and wild
peonies form carpets of incomparable hues where
the cliff ends and the land shows itself fertile and
kind. In the spring even the ponds and clay pits are
covered with a thousand little white flowers that
move us to adore and love the Sower. Rosemary,
pepper plants, honeysuckle, penny-royals, in the
moor and in the brakes, fill the air with the fragrance of countless, pleasing, and penetrating aro-
mas. It is the same perfume that comes from the
fresh, clean clothing of the girls of the village when

on Sunday morning they open their trunks and don their simple dresses.

The Cabeço was then the most beautiful of all places. It was for that reason also that the three children liked to go there. "On the side of that hill," says Lúcia, "there were many and various kinds of flowers, among them the lilies we were very fond of. And when in the evening Jacinta waited for me on the path, she brought me a lily or, if this were lacking, any other flower. She then plucked off its petals and scattered them over me." Spring and early summer bring other flowers: the white and pink blossoms of the wrack, the wild flax with its yellow and pink petals, and the wild gypsophila with its little flowers found at every step. We have seen already how Jacinta liked to take the part of an angel and return with an armful of flowers to throw at Lúcia, her cherished friend before and after the apparitions.

O flowers of Fatima! What intimate converse with the ingenuous and candid soul of Jacinta! What memories of her tender colloquies with you will forever remain hovering throughout that beloved solitude!

CHAPTER 7

Jacinta— The Shepherdess

Jacinta entered upon the life of a shepherdess. There were not many sheep under her charge, for she was very small and could not take care of many. For that reason each one had a name either inherited from its predecessor or given it by Jacinta. The beautiful mornings invited one to go out. As soon as the little shepherdess appeared, her mother or her sisters came to help her lead out the flock. The sheep ran to meet her, to get the sweetmeats which she usually shared with them.

"We won over the little sheep," says Lúcia, "by distributing among them our own lunches; for that reason we could play in peace when we arrived at the pasture, since they would not go far away from us."

As soon as little Jacinta, graceful and elegant, dressed in striped skirt and apron, appeared with her little satchel at the door to remove the bolt, the sheep immediately came out to meet her. It seems that I can even now see her walking behind the flock which knew and loved her well. The three children came together at a prearranged spot, whence they went happily on their way. The pasture wound in and out over the countryside. Now and again they would go toward the east, then descend toward the north, climb the narrow path to the highway that circled the village of Fatima, leaving the church to the right, and finally come to the summit, radiant with joy. The slope of the hill climbed up to the windmills, whence the eye, looking to the west, south, and east, could see the already well-known panorama, with the Cova da Iria, the Lomba d'Égua, the Moita, and the heights of St. Catherine of the Mountain to the northeast. Their eyes were closed to everything else before this magnificent spectacle, old yet ever new in the beauty which is reborn in every fresh glance of the beholder. Neither custom nor habit could dull the beautiful panorama—one of the most beautiful that the Portuguese land has to offer.

Behind the hedge of mountain crests, still blinking from the sleep of the night, the sun timidly cast forth its rays, making the very dust sparkle in the morning glow. After a night spent in sleep over the brooks and meadows, the mist grew restless in the valleys and woke with a start. Toward the north and the south lay the sad, dark green mantle of pine trees without end. Nearby, precipices dug almost vertically into the sides of the mountain, like huge wine vats. In front lay the rich tilled plains of Ourém. In magnificent majesty rose a castle, like a sentinel, to defend the Christian land from the invading Moors. Battered by the centuries, it stood against the morning sky, gilded by the sun, leaving the horizon in a mysterious shadow. On the other side ran the fertile brook, born at its feet, flowing down through Vila Nova and Ceissa, hurrying to empty into the Nabão. Like a mother with rich breasts, it gives up its water little by little, day and night, enriching the people on the banks, who suck it dry.

As the sun arose, nature awakened; the meadows became alive, the cocks crowed in the backyards, and the flock scattered to nibble at the tender blades of grass. A thrill of life animated the earth—the prayer of the morning. The soul of the shepherds, the soul of Jacinta, rose to God, the Creator of so great a beauty. First came the prayer of the spirit in the depths of the soul. Enraptured by the grandeur of the spectacle, she prayed and sang and loved to hear the echo repeat her cherished prayer.

"Jacinta loved to hear the echo of her voice in the depth of the valleys," says Lúcia. "For that reason, one of our entertainments was to sit on the largest cliff on the summit of the mountain, and to pronounce names in a loud voice. The name that echoed back best was the name Maria, and Jacinta would at times recite the whole Hail Mary, repeating the following word only when the preceding one had finished its echo. We also loved to sing hymns and popular songs. Unfortunately we knew far more of the latter. Jacinta preferred the 'Salve Nobre Padroeira,' the 'Virgem Pura,' and the 'Anjos Cantai Comigo.'"

During the hot months the flocks would go out earlier, before sunrise, for afterward the heat prevented the sheep from eating. They would get tired on the way, and return panting, with lowered heads—a sad sight to see. For the old sheep, it would not matter, but how could the little lambs endure it—they are so lovely! It pained one to see them suffer. For that reason, "Jacinta loved to catch the little white lambs and hold them in her lap, embrace them, kiss them, and in the evening bring them back home on her back lest they should get tired. One day as we came home, she placed herself in the midst of the flock.

"'What are you doing in the midst of the flock?' I asked.

"'I want to be like Our Lord, who, on the holy card which they gave me, is standing like this in the midst of very many sheep, carrying one in His arms.'"

Pastoral life has charms beyond our imagination. But at times, on deserted mountains and in the meadows, the life is rough, and only very strong men can endure it. Hence shepherds from the fields and woods of Alentejo and from the heights of the Serra da Estrela and of the Gardunha stay with their flocks day and night for a long time. On the slopes of the Serra d'Aire it is more human, more varied, and more homelike. The shepherds come home every day with their flocks. Both shepherd and sheep have their shelter in the village. Not as rough and hard as that of other regions, here the life of the shepherd offers greater advantages for the growing child. It is not abandoned, but supported. Its milieu is the family, and parents and brothers watch over it, follow it, guide it, and, if necessary, punish it.

For that reason, generally, no one is a shepherd by profession but only by way of entertaining and occupying the children, while drawing some profit from the work. The mountain people are ordinarily very thrifty. It is likely that they have this marked tendency to be economical because they are reared from infancy to a practical, useful life. The shepherd has to know his land very well, with all its nooks and corners and conditions of vegetation, and to be abreast of the news of his small world—the shepherd world—so that he may know where the best pasture land is to be found for his flocks. He has to be discreet and reserved. Hence there is a precocious development of intelligence, which led the priests even at that time to give Communion to the children before they were seven years old, as was the case with Lúcia. Jacinta was truly intelligent and bright. This fact is attested by various events in her life, as well as by those who knew her. The following words of Lúcia may illustrate the point:

"It is apropos here to tell a story which shows how Jacinta sought to escape the persons who visited her after the apparitions and how ably she could do it. One day as we were going to Fatima, we saw a group of ladies and gentlemen getting out of an automobile. There was no doubt that they were looking for us, but we could not run without being spotted, and so we went ahead in the hope of not being recognized. When the group reached us, they asked whether we knew the shepherds to whom Our Lady had appeared. We answered that we did. Did we know where they lived? We gave them all the directions necessary to get there, and then we ran to hide in the fields behind the hedges. Jacinta was so happy at the success of this ruse that she said, 'We will always do this whenever we are not recognized.'"

The way she learned her catechism, her remarks, her answers, her conversation—all this has been preserved for us by her cousin. They reveal that Jacinta possessed a balanced mind even somewhat superior to the average child of her age.

8

Heavenly Visitor

The charm of the old legends whose ingenuous simplicity and candidness delighted us is fast vanishing. Why cling to legend when the actuality before our eyes is powerful and thrilling? Events such as those in the lives of the saints, as well as their converse with heaven, are repeated in our day. Angels in human form still come down to us. Such intercourse is a reality even today. The books of Genesis, Tobias, and Kings bear witness that from the very beginning messengers from heaven have been sent to us. Not even the coming of the Divine Word, and His presence upon earth as one of us, has put an end to the climbing and descending on Jacob's Ladder.

The Annunciation, the good news of the birth of Jesus given to the shepherds, the flight into Egypt, and the return to Palestine were all due to angelic intermediation. Angels ministered unto the Lord in the desert. An angel comforted Him in the Garden of Olives. Angels appeared near the sepulcher after the Resurrection and talked with the women, and were also present on the Mount of Olives after the Ascension. Holy Mother Church among her feasts has one dedicated to the apparition of Saint Michael on Mount Gargano.

The territory around Aljustrel was witness to the angelic colloquies which we are about to narrate.

The horizon of the Cova da Iria is broken on all sides by a chain of hills, enlivened by the rhythmic wheeling of the sails of the windmills. Looking from the shrine to the southwest one sees a windmill crowning a green-crested hill. It is the windmill of the Cabeço. Seen from the shrine at a distance of more than a mile, the Cabeço seems insignificant, but when seen in its proper surroundings, it becomes for the people of Aljustrel a protection against the wind, and for the little ones it assumes the proportions of a lofty mountain. It is separated from the village by Valinhos. At its foot, facing the village, lies the Pregueira. The parish is half-way up the hill toward Eira da Pedra.

This same Cabeço came to take a place of importance in the life of the seers. The details of the apparitions of the angel were known at the time of the first edition of *Jacinta,* but it was not thought convenient just then to announce them to the public. Sister Maria Lúcia de Jesus was consulted personally, inquiries and observations were made, and it cannot be doubted that the apparitions were real and authentic, so great, so deep, and so enduring was the effect produced on the souls of the three children. It is not to be wondered that God should want to prepare them in this way by union of suffering for the events which were to follow shortly. Sister Maria Lúcia de Jesus writes about the apparitions:

"The time seems to have been between April and October of 1916. I cannot give the exact dates, for at that time I could not count the years, nor the months, nor even the days of the week. However, it seems to me that it must have been in the spring of 1916 that the angel appeared to us at the Cabeço for the first time. At this time Francisco and Jacinta asked and obtained, as I have told Your Excellency, permission from their parents to pasture their flocks. We then agreed to feed our sheep on the property of my uncle and of my parents, so that we might not be on the mountain with the other shepherds.

"One day we went with our sheep to a field of my parents which is situated at the bottom of the mountain facing the east. That property is known as the Casa Velha. There, by mid morning, it began to drizzle somewhat heavily. We climbed the slope of the mountain, followed by our little sheep, looking for a cliff to use for a shelter. It was then for the first time we entered that blessed cavern. It is in the midst of an olive orchard which belonged to my godfather, Anastasio. From there we could see the village where I was born, my parents' house, the parishes of the Casa Velha and Eira da Pedra. The olive grove, which belongs to various owners, continues until it is blended with these small villages.

"There we spent the day, even though the rain had stopped and the sun had appeared beautiful and clear. We ate our lunch and said the rosary. After the rosary we began to play. We had been playing only for a few minutes when a strong wind shook the trees and made us raise our eyes to see what was going on, for the day was serene.

"We began to see at a distance over the trees which spread toward the east, a light whiter than snow, with the form of a transparent youth more brilliant than crystal transfixed by the rays of the sun. As he approached we were able to distinguish his features. We were spellbound and half-wrapped in ecstasy, and could not utter one word. As he neared us, he said, 'Do not fear. I am the Angel of Peace. Pray with me.' And kneeling, he bowed his head to the ground. Moved by a supernatural impulse, we imitated him, and repeated the words which we heard him pronounce: 'My God, I believe, I adore, I hope, and I love you. I ask you for pardon for those who do not believe, who do not adore, who do not pray, and who do not love you.' After repeating this three times, he arose and said, 'Pray thus. The hearts of Jesus and Mary are attentive to the voice of your supplication.' And then he disappeared.

"The atmosphere of the supernatural that enveloped us was so intense that we were almost unaware of our own existence for a great space of time. We remained in the position in which he had left us, repeating constantly the same prayer. The presence of God was felt so intensely and so intimately that we dared not speak, even among ourselves.

"On the following day, we felt our souls still enveloped by that atmosphere, which disappeared only gradually. None of us thought of speaking of this apparition or of recommending that it be kept secret. The apparition itself imposed the secret. It was so intimate that it was not easy to refer to it in the slightest way. It made a great impression upon us, perhaps because it was the first such manifestation.

"The second apparition must have taken place in midsummer. In those days when the heat was oppressive, we usually took our flocks home in the middle of the morning to keep them sheltered until late afternoon. We would spend the siesta hours under the shade of the trees which surrounded the well at the bottom of the garden in the Arneiro. Suddenly one day we saw the same Angel near us.

"'What are you doing?' he asked. 'Pray, pray much. The hearts of Jesus and Mary have designs of mercy upon you. Offer prayers and sacrifices constantly to the Almighty.'

"'How are we to sacrifice ourselves?' I questioned.

"'In everything you can, offer a sacrifice as an act of reparation for the sins by which He is offended, and of supplication for the conversion of sinners. Thus draw peace upon our country. I am its guardian angel, the Angel of Portugal. Above all, accept and endure with submission the suffering which Our Lord will send you.'

"These words of the Angel were engraved on our hearts like a light which made us understand who God was, how He loved us and wanted to be loved, and the value of sacrifice, how pleasing it was to Him, and how because of it He converted sinners. For that reason, from that moment on we began to offer to Our Lord everything which mortified us, but without wandering about in search of other mortifications and penances except for spending hour after hour prostrate on the earth repeating the prayer which the Angel had taught us.

"The third apparition must have been in October, or toward the end of September, for we no longer spent the hours of siesta at home. We went out from the Pregueira (this is a small olive orchard which belongs to my parents) to the cavern, going around the mountain on the side of Aljustrel and Casa Velha. There we said the rosary and the prayer which the Angel had taught us in the first apparition. Then he appeared for the third time, carrying in his hand a chalice, and above it a host from which a few drops of blood fell into the chalice. Leaving the chalice and the host suspended in mid air, he prostrated himself on the earth, and repeated three times this prayer: 'Most Holy Trinity, Father, Son, and Holy Ghost, I adore You profoundly, and I offer to you the most precious Body and Blood, Soul and Divinity of Jesus Christ, present in all the tabernacles of the earth, in reparation for the outrages, sacrileges, and indifferences with which He Himself is offended. And through the infinite merits of His most Sacred Heart, and of the Immaculate Heart of Mary, I beseech you for the conversion of poor sinners.'

"Then raising himself, he again took the chalice and the host. He gave me the host, and the contents of the chalice to Jacinta and Francisco, saying at the same time, 'Eat and drink the Body and Blood of Jesus Christ, horribly outraged by ungrateful men. Make reparation for their crimes, and console your God.'

"Again he prostrated himself on the ground, and with us he repeated three times the same prayer, 'Most Holy Trinity, etc.,' and then disappeared.

"Impelled by the power of the supernatural which enveloped us, we imitated the Angel in everything. We prostrated ourselves like him, and repeated the prayers he said. The awareness of the presence of God was so intense that it absorbed us and almost annihilated us completely. It seemed to deprive us of the use of our bodily senses for a great space of time. In those days we performed our physical activities as though compelled by that same supernatural being. The peace and happiness which we felt was great and intimate, with our souls completely concentrated on God. The physical weakness which prostrated us was also great. I do not know why, but the apparitions of Our Lady produced in us very different effects. The same intimate joy, the same peace and happiness were present, but instead of that bodily exhaustion we felt a certain physical strength. In place of that annihilation before the Divine Presence, we felt exultation and joy; in place of the difficulty in speaking, we felt a certain communicative enthusiasm. But notwithstanding all those sentiments, we felt inspired to be silent, especially concerning certain things."

These facts contain many lessons. Let us allow at least some of them to remain well-impressed upon our hearts. Nations, like individuals, have their guardian angels. Let us recommend our country to her own. If during life we owe to our holy angel so many inspirations, so many good thoughts, so great and such assiduous protection, why do we not recommend this devotion and inculcate it warmly in the souls of children, whom it is our duty to form? It is good to know that against the attacks of the tempter and against the assaults of the passions and the seductions of the world, there is someone by our side, ordered by God to defend us, to help us, to guard us night and day.

To children and adults, to ourselves and others let us make it understood and felt more and more that the Blessed Eucharist is the font and origin of all Christian greatness, for in it we receive the very Author of Grace, Christ Jesus.

Consecrated by Sorrow

Thus had been spent "seven years of Jacinta's life," writes Lúcia, "when there dawned, beautiful and smiling as so many other days, the 13th day of May, 1917. By chance, if anything happens by chance in the designs of Providence, we chose on that day to take our flocks to the property called Cova da Iria, which belonged to my parents, where we were wont to go at other times. To reach the pasture land chosen for that day, we had to cross a moor, thus doubling the distance we usually had to travel. We walked slowly to let the sheep graze on the way, and arrived there about noon."

They were playing on the summit where the new church now stands, while the flock was grazing around them. Suddenly, "we saw the reflection of a light which we thought to be lightning, but because we were accustomed to see lightning only when there was thunder, we concluded that a storm was approaching."

The weather was beautiful that day, but because May thunderstorms are famous in Portugal, Lúcia, the oldest of the three, thought it best to return home. Having summoned the flock, they were already turning homeward, and were passing in front of a small holm oak, where now stands the Chapel of Apparitions, when a brilliant light caught their attention. Standing there, above the holm oak, was Our Lady.

"Within the light which enveloped her, we could see a Lady, perfect in every way. We were already so near as to be somewhat within the light which surrounded her."

She spoke to them. Afterward they resolved to keep the vision a secret, but Jacinta was restless, and when she arrived home, she could not contain herself. Perturbed at this, Lúcia reprimanded and later scolded her, saying that she was to blame for all the sorrows and persecutions which they had to suffer.

Thus Lúcia writes: "Before beginning to narrate what I remember of the new period of the life of Jacinta, it is perhaps best for me to say a few things concerning the manifestations of Our Lady, which we had agreed never to tell anybody, in order to explain whence Jacinta absorbed so much love of Jesus, of suffering, and of sinners, for whose salvation she made many sacrifices. It was she who, unable to contain within herself so much joy, broke the contract which bound us to maintain secrecy. For on that very afternoon while, still wrapt in wonder, we remained pensive, Jacinta would exclaim now and then with great enthusiasm, 'Oh, what a beautiful Lady!'

"'I'm willing to bet,' I would say, 'that you are going to tell it to somebody.'

"'Oh, no I won't,' she exclaimed, 'don't you worry about it.'

"On the following day, after her brother had brought me the news that she had revealed it, Jacinta listened to my accusations without making any response.

"'Do you see? I thought so!' I said to her.

"'I have something inside that does not let me keep silence,' she answered, with tears in her eyes.

"'Now, don't cry, and don't tell anything else to anyone about what the Lady told us.'

"'I have already told.'

"'What did you tell?'

"'I told that the Lady promised to take us to heaven.'

"'Why did you have to say that?'

"'Forgive me. I won't tell any more to anybody.'

"When we arrived at the pasture the next day, Jacinta sat thoughtfully on a rock.

"'Jacinta, come over and play with us,' I said.

"'I don't want to play today,' she replied.

"'Why not?'

"'Because I remember that the Lady told us to say the rosary and to make sacrifices for the conversion of sinners. When we say the rosary from now on, we have to say the whole Hail Mary and the whole Our Father. And how are we to make sacrifices?'"

The news began to spread among their friends and neighbors, perhaps through the brothers of the little seers who spoke scoffingly of the event. From month to month the number of those who wanted to assist at those heavenly manifestations increased. Religious and civil authorities took cognizance of the case, and proceeded according to their ideas and convictions. The parish priest, Father Ferreira, prudently withdrew. The Administrator of the district concerned himself with the matter and showed his authority. The apparitions of Cova da Iria became public property as the news spread far and wide.

In October of 1917, 70,000 persons assembled at Cova da Iria. Newspaper men were on hand, eager for a story, while unbelievers came to scoff. There were some conversions, for in the sun and in the sky appeared phenomena which science could not explain. Even after the last apparition pilgrimages to the place which the seers affirmed had been sanctified by the corporeal presence of the most Blessed Virgin, continued. Such is, in briefest outline, the summary of what took place.

Little did the children realize how many sacrifices and tribulations the Lady was to require of them. Rather, perhaps, they knew they were to suffer but would not tell anyone. Only now and then is a bit of the veil lifted from this secret.

"These are the words which the Blessed Virgin told me on that day, and which we agreed never to reveal.

"After having told us that we would go to heaven, the Lady asked: 'Do you wish to offer

yourselves to God, to endure all the sufferings
which He wants to send you, as an act of reparation for the sins by which He is offended and as a
supplication for the conversion of sinners?'

"'Yes, we do,' was our answer.

"'You are, then, going to have much to suffer,
but the grace of God will be your comfort.'

"On the 13th of June, the Feast of St. Anthony
was being celebrated in our parish. It was the custom on that day to take out the flocks early in
the morning and then to bring them back to the
corral at nine o'clock, before going to the fiesta.
My mother and my sisters, who knew how much
I liked to go, kept saying to me: 'We shall see now
whether you pass up the fiesta to go to the Cova
da Iria to speak to the Lady.'"

The family did not believe; and, as Lúcia later
revealed, the scoffing of her family and their doubt
caused her much suffering. It was the general opinion at home that the children were lying. Lúcia's
mother tried at all costs to convince her of that,
and even went so far as to take her to the pastor
to have her confess her lie. It was a terrible siege.
Only a supernatural strength could sustain them.
Lúcia tells it vividly more than once:

"In the meantime, the news of the happening had spread. My mother was beginning to worry and insisted that I contradict myself. One day, before I went out with the flock, she endeavored to force me to admit that I had lied. To attain her aim she spared neither caresses nor threats, not even the broomstick. She received as an answer merely dumb silence or the confirmation of what I had already said. She told me to take out the flock and to consider well during the day that she had never permitted her children to lie, and much less would she now allow an untruth of this kind. She warned me that in the evening she would force me to go to those persons whom I had deceived and admit that I had lied, asking their forgiveness for it. I departed with my little sheep, and found my friends already waiting for me. Seeing my tears, they asked me the reason.

"I told them what had taken place and added, 'Now tell me what to do. My mother wants me to say that I lied, but how can I say that?'

"Francisco then said to Jacinta, 'Do you see? You are to blame for all this. Why did you have to tell!'

"The poor child knelt in tears before me, and raising her hands asked us for forgiveness. 'I did wrong,' she said in her tears, 'but I will never again tell a thing to anybody.'

"It may be asked who taught her to perform such an act of humility. I do not know. Perhaps it was because she had seen her brothers ask forgiveness of their parents on the eve of their First Communion, or perhaps because Jacinta was the one, as it seems to me, to whom the Blessed Virgin communicated a greater abundance of grace, knowledge of God, and virtue.

"The turn of events worried my mother more and more. As a result she made another effort to force me to confess that I had lied. One morning she called me and said that she was going to take me to Father Ferreira. She commanded me: 'When you arrive there, kneel down and tell him that you lied, and ask his forgiveness.'

"I was in great anxiety, for I could see that my mother was worried. She wanted in any event to force me, as she said, to admit my lie. I wanted to satisfy her, but I could find no way of doing it without lying. From the cradle she had infused in her children a great horror for lying, and severely punished anyone who told the least untruth.

"She used to say, 'I have always managed to have my children tell the truth, and am I now going to permit something like this in my youngest child? This is a thing of no small importance, this lie which has fooled so many people!'

"After these complaints she would turn to me and say, 'You may say whatever you wish; but you set those people right by confessing that you lied, or I will lock you in a room where you will not be able to see so much as the light of the sun.'

"My sisters took my mother's side, and so all around me there was an atmosphere of real contempt and scorn. Then I would think of former times and ask myself where was that affection which only a little while ago my family had entertained for me. My only relief was in tears shed before God as I offered Him my sacrifice; my only alleviation was to be alone in a solitary corner where I would weep to my heart's content. I began to feel annoyed even with the company of my cousins, and for that reason I began to hide myself from them. Poor children! At times they would look for me and call me by name while I was near to them but wouldn't answer, sometimes in a corner where they had not been able to look.

"One day my mother, having again resolved to oblige me to retract, decided to take me on the following day to see Father Ferreira, so that I might confess to him that I had lied, ask his forgiveness, and perform the penances which his Reverence might think well to impose upon me. This time the attack was so strong that I did not know what to do. I passed by the house of my uncle, told Jacinta, who was still in bed, what was taking place, and then followed my mother. On the road she continued to lecture to me.

"At a certain point I said to her, trembling, 'But mother, how can I say that I did not see, when I did see?'

"She was silent. During the Mass, I offered my sacrifice to God. Then I crossed the atrium behind my mother, and climbed the stairs leading to the veranda of the parish house.

"As I climbed the first step, she turned to me and said, 'Don't vex me any more. Now tell Father that you lied, so that he may be able on Sunday to announce in the church that it was all a lie, and thus put an end to everything. How can this continue, so many people running to Cova da Iria to pray in front of a holm oak!'

"Thereupon she knocked at the door. The priest's sister saw us in, inviting us to sit on a bench and wait a while. At last Father came, asked us into his study, and signalled my mother to sit on the bench. Then he called me to his desk. When I heard his Reverence interrogate me with calmness and even with amiability, I was surprised. He questioned me in great detail, with all seriousness and politeness, using a few artifices to see whether I would contradict myself or modify my statements. Finally he dismissed us with a shrug of his shoulders as though he meant to say, 'I do not know what to say or what to do about all this.'"

To explain the insistence with which Senhora Maria Rosa tried to force her daughter to contradict herself, we shall bring this chapter to a close with the appreciation which Sister Maria Lúcia de Jesus herself had made of her mother. It may seem a matter of little importance, but it throws a singular light upon her attitude.

"My poor mother worried more and more as she saw the multitudes of people coming from everywhere. She would say, 'These poor people coming here are certainly fooled by your deceits! I really do not know what to do to set them right.'

"One day, a poor man who boasted of making fun of us, of insulting us, and even of beating us asked my mother, 'Well, now, Senhora Maria Rosa, what have you to say about the visions of your daughter?'

"'I do not know,' she answered, 'It seems to me that she is nothing but a fake who has succeeded in fooling half the world.'

"'Don't say that too loudly, lest someone may kill her. It seems that there are some who have a real grudge against her, and would like to do it.'

"'Oh, I don't care, so long as they force her to tell the truth. I will always tell the truth whether it be against my children or against anyone else, even against myself.'

"It really was so. My mother always told the truth even if it were against herself. We, her children, owe her this good example."

Even though Jacinta did not meet with such a great struggle at home, we have from the description of Lúcia's tribulations an idea of how much Jacinta herself had to suffer because of the apparitions.

10

Torment
of Doubt

The interview with Father Ferreira caused quite a commotion. Mother and sisters joined in to torment poor Lúcia. Jacinta and her mother lived a little more quietly at this time. As soon as the sisters of Lúcia learned through their mother that the priest had called for her, they began to frighten her.

"My sisters took my mother's side, and invented a number of threats to frighten me concerning the interview with the pastor.

"I informed Jacinta and her brother of what was taking place, and they answered, 'We also are going. Father Ferreira asked my mother to take us there, but she has told us nothing about those things. Have patience. If they beat us, we shall suffer for the love of Our Lord and for sinners!'

"When His Reverence interrogated Jacinta, she lowered her head and answered only two or three words. As we went away, I asked her, 'Why didn't you want to answer Father Ferreira?'

"'Because I promised to tell nothing more to anyone.'"

Inasmuch as Lúcia was the oldest, the pastor gave her more careful consideration and advice. At the end of the questioning, the doubt continued. Was it a truly prudent doubt, or was it merely superficial? Whatever it was, the attitude of the Reverend Father Manuel Marques Ferreira was the only one which a person in a responsible position could assume. Revealing for a moment his thoughts, he said at the close of the visit:

"It does not appear to me to be a revelation from heaven. Ordinarily when such things take place, Our Lady orders those souls to whom she reveals herself to tell the happenings to their confessor, or to the pastor. But this one, on the contrary, withholds as much as possible. This could be a trick of the devil—we shall see. The future will tell what we must think."

This remark was like a bombshell, for Lúcia was docile and full of respect for the clergy. The opinion of Father Ferreira troubled her soul.

"How much this reflection made me suffer only Our Lord knows, for He alone can penetrate our inmost heart. I began then to question whether the manifestations were not from the devil who sought by this means to damn me. Since I had heard that the devil always brought with him conflict and disorder, I began to think that truly since I had seen these things I had had neither joy nor rest in our home. In great anguish, I revealed my doubt to my cousin.

"Jacinta answered, 'Oh, no, it is not from the devil. They say that the devil is very ugly and lives under the ground in hell, but that Lady is so beautiful! Besides, we saw her go up to heaven.'

"Our Lord allowed this to allay my doubt somewhat, but during this month of June I lost all enthusiasm for the practise of sacrifice and mortification. I even considered whether or not I would end by telling I had lied and so finish everything.

"Jacinta and Francisco would tell me, 'Don't do that! Don't you see this would be a lie, and that to lie is a sin?'"

The conviction and the courage of the two younger children were a comfort to her, even though fleeting. Now she had to wrestle with a dream which made a horrible impression upon her imagination.

"While in this condition I had a dream which increased the darkness of my spirit. I saw the devil, who, laughing for having fooled me, endeavored to drag me to hell. Seeing myself in his clutches, I began to shriek in such a way, calling for Our Lady, that I woke my mother, who brought me back to my senses by asking me what was the matter. I do not remember what I answered her. What I do remember is that on that night I could sleep no longer, since I was paralyzed with fear. This dream left a cloud of real fear and affliction in my soul.

"The 13th day of July was close at hand, but I hesitated to go to the place of the apparitions I thought to myself, 'If it is the devil, why should I go there to see him? If they ask me why I do not go, I shall say that I am afraid that it may be the devil who appears to us, and for that reason I do not go. Let Francisco and Jacinta do as they please; as for me, I am not returning to the Cova da Iria.'

"I made the resolution and was bent on putting it into practise. On the 12th of July in the afternoon people began to gather for the events of the following day. I called Jacinta and Francisco and informed them of my resolution, but they replied, 'We are going. The Lady ordered us to go there.'

"Jacinta volunteered to speak to the Lady, but she was sorry that I was not going and began to cry. I asked her why she cried.

"'Because you do not want to go,' she answered.

"'No, I am not going. Look, if the Lady asks you for me, tell her that I am not going because I am afraid it may be the devil.'

"And I left them to hide myself, so that I would not have to speak to the people who were seeking to question me. When I arrived home that night, my mother reprimanded me. She thought that during all this time I had been playing with the children of the neighborhood whereas I had spent the time hidden behind the hedge of the property of a neighbor next to our Arneiro.

"'What a beautiful saint she turned out to be!' she exclaimed. 'All the time she has left from watching the sheep she spends playing where no one can find her.'

"On the following day, as the hour for leaving approached, I felt suddenly impelled to go by a strange force which was impossible to resist. I went, and on the way passed by the house of my uncle to see if Jacinta were still there. I found her in her room with her brother Francisco, kneeling at the bedside and weeping.

"'Aren't you going?' I asked them.

"'Without you, we don't dare go. Come with us.'

"'I'm coming,' I answered.

"Then with a joyful air they came with me. The people had gathered in great numbers waiting for us on the roads, so that it was only with difficulty that we arrived there. It was on this day that Our Lady deigned to reveal to us the secret, and once again she counseled us to sacrifice ourselves for sinners."

The doubt had vanished. There was again peace in her soul, but greater exterior tribulations were about to begin. Perhaps one or another of our readers may also have been tormented by doubt concerning the seers and the apparitions. Let us, therefore, examine those doubts.

These three children belonged to the normal type of mountain children; being peasants, their features were more or less hardened, their brows were tanned by the sun and the wind, their build was short and stocky and they were very healthy. Jacinta was strong, and had a hearty constitution. So had Lúcia. Francisco, before he contracted pneumonia, was perhaps the strongest of the three. This, then, removes the possibility of their having a nervous temperament, which is not found in the family even today.

How then explain the firmness of their assertions, and the perfect agreement of the testimonies of the three under the close questionings to which they were subjected? Is it wild imagination? Hardly that, for they could not read. Only on Sunday afternoon or on long evenings would Lúcia's mother spend some time in reading to her children the lives of the saints. Then, the children themselves furnished proof to the contrary. If it were a question of imagination, they would hardly shrink from speaking of such beautiful things, nor would they agree to be silent. The life of the three continued in its external aspect to be perfectly normal. Is it a farce, then? How could it be, when the entire family attacked the children bitterly, or at least maintained a stubborn silence? On the part of the pastor, it would be ridiculous to imagine any interference, since he is accused of being against the apparitions.

Let us open the Gospel and see what Our Lord has to say. "By their fruits you shall know them." The radical change in their life of piety, their development and progress in virtue, the pious death of Francisco and Jacinta, the information which Lúcia gives us of the new Jacinta presented throughout this work, are good fruits. We have to conclude, then, that the causes—the trees which bore the fruit—were also good. The sweet memory of the beautiful Lady, which remained with them, filled their souls, united and transformed them, and was like a ray of the sun illumining the mist of doubt which hovered like a hellish torment over the souls of these three children, who were humble, simple, and sincere.

This is how Sister Maria Lúcia de Jesus in a letter of December 5, 1937, to His Excellency the Most Reverend Bishop of Leiria, refers to the heavenly vision of twenty years before:

"In the holy cards which I have seen, Our Lady appears to have two mantles. It seems to me that if I could paint, even though I would never be capable of painting her as she is, since I know that is impossible, just as it is impossible to describe her—I would put only one tunic, the simplest and whitest possible, with the mantle falling from her head to the soles of her feet. Since I could not paint the light and beauty which adorned her, I would suppress all the ornaments with the exception of a golden thread around the mantle. This gold thread was outstanding, like a ray of the sun, but shining even more brightly. The description is far from the reality, but I can express myself in no better way."

A Great Atoning Soul

We now enter upon the most beautiful phase of Jacinta's life and upon the most important chapter of this little work. Jacinta is revealed to us in the following pages as raised by God to the heights of a life of reparation. "But how are we to make sacrifices?" Jacinta asked thoughtfully after the Lady had announced to them that they must sacrifice themselves for sinners. And then, taking the Lady's message to heart, she never missed an opportunity to suffer for their conversion. Lúcia writes: "One day we saw the two Moita children who used to go begging from door to door, and Jacinta cried, 'Let's give our lunch to those poor children for the conversion of sinners.' And she ran to give it to them.

When later in the day she told me she was hungry I suggested that we eat some acorns even though they were green. Thereupon Francisco climbed a holm oak to fill his pockets, but Jacinta reminded us that for a sacrifice, we could eat the bitter acorns of the oak trees rather than those of the holm oaks, and so we had a delicious repast that afternoon. Jacinta took this as one of her habitual sacrifices: to eat the acorn of the oak trees or the olives of the olive trees.

"One day I told her, 'Jacinta, don't eat that; it is too bitter.'

"'It is just because it is bitter that I am eating it, for the conversion of sinners,' she replied.

"Our fasts did not consist only in these practises. We agreed that whenever we met the poor we would give them our lunch. As a result those poor children made it a point to meet us every day on the road; as soon as we spotted them Jacinta would run to give them our daily nourishment with as much satisfaction as if she would never miss it. In those days we lived on the kernels of fir-cones, on roots of shrubs (especially those of the little yellow flowers which contain a little berry about the size of an olive), on berries, mushrooms, and a few other things which we gathered from the roots of pine trees, the names of which I do not recall, or on fruit, if there was any on the property belonging to our parents.

"Jacinta seemed insatiable in the practise of sacrifice. One day a neighbor offered my mother a good pasture for our sheep, but it was too far away and we were in the midst of summer. However, my mother accepted the offer and sent me there. Since there was a pond nearby where the flock could drink, she told me that we had better spend the siesta there in the shade of the trees. On the way we met our dear poor children and Jacinta ran to give them our lunch.

"The day was beautiful, but the sun was scorching and in that deserted and arid place it seemed to set everything on fire. We were burning with thirst, and there was not a drop of water to drink. At first we offered the suffering with generosity for the conversion of sinners but after midday we could not persist. Then I offered to go to a house not far away to ask for a little water. They accepted the proposal, so I went to the door of a little old woman who gave me not only a pitcher of water but also a piece of bread which I accepted with gratitude and ran to share it with my friends.

"When I gave the pitcher to Francisco and asked him to drink, he replied, 'I don't want any.'

"'Why not?'

"'I want to suffer for the conversion of sinners.'

"'You drink, Jacinta.'

"'I also want to offer this sacrifice for sinners.'

"Then I poured the water in the hollow of a rock so that the sheep might drink it and returned the pitcher to the owner. The heat was becoming intense; the locusts and the crickets joined their chirping to the croaking of the frogs in the nearby pond, and made an unbearable noise. Jacinta, weakened by hunger and thirst, said to me with that simplicity which was natural to her: 'Tell the crickets and the frogs to be quiet. I have an awful headache.'

"Then Francisco asked her, 'Don't you want to suffer this for sinners?'

"The poor child pressed her hands to her head and answered, 'Yes, I do. Let them sing.'

"We occasionally made it a point to spend nine days or a month without drinking. Once we made this sacrifice in the middle of August when the heat was suffocating. While we were returning from saying our rosary in the Cova da Iria we approached a pond called Carreira, and Jacinta said: 'Oh, I am so thirsty, and my head aches terribly . . . I am going to drink a little of this water.'

"'Not of this water,' I hastened to intervene. 'My mother does not want us to drink it because it will make us sick. Let's ask Senhora Maria dos Anjos for a little.' (She was one of our neighbors who had married and was living there in a small house.)

"'No, I don't want that good water; I would rather drink from the pond because instead of offering the thirst to our Lord, I would offer Him the sacrifice of drinking this dirty water.'

"As a matter of fact this water was foul; several persons washed their clothes in it, and animals came there to drink and to bathe. Wisely my mother warned us not to drink of it.

"At times Jacinta would say, 'Our Lord must be happy with our sacrifices, because I am so thirsty; but I don't want to drink; I want to suffer for His love.'"

Not everybody in the village was left undisturbed by the apparitions. There were women who spoke of nothing else and who could never accept the fact that such things could be believed.

"Some of those women," writes Lúcia, "when they met me, gave vent to their disgust by insulting me and at times by dismissing me with a couple of kicks. Jacinta and Francisco rarely shared in these caresses which heaven sent me, because their parents would not permit anyone to touch them. But they suffered in seeing me suffer, and frequently tears bathed their faces when they saw me afflicted or mortified. One day, Jacinta told me, 'I wish my parents were like yours, so that these people might beat me also. In that way I would have more sacrifices to offer to Our Lord.'

"However she knew how to use well the occasions of mortifying herself. One day, while we were sitting at the gate of my uncle's house, we noticed that several persons were approaching. Francisco and I immediately ran, each one to his own room to hide under the bed, but Jacinta said, 'I am not going to hide; I am going to offer this sacrifice to Our Lord.'

"These persons approached, spoke with her, waited for a long time while they looked for me, and finally went away. Then I left my hiding-place, and asked her, 'What did you answer when they asked you about us?'

"'I answered nothing. I lowered my head, fixed my eyes on the ground, and said nothing. I always act like that when I don't want to tell the truth. I would never lie, because a lie is a sin.'

"In fact it was her custom to follow this procedure, and it was useless to question her further, for she would not give the least response. We would not ordinarily make sacrifices of this kind if we could avoid it.

"One day we were playing at the oft-mentioned well. Nearby, Jacinta's mother had a grapevine. She cut a few clusters and brought them to us, but Jacinta never forgot her sinners. 'We won't eat them,' she said, 'We will rather offer this sacrifice for sinners.' Then she ran out with the grapes and gave them to the children who were playing in the street. She returned radiant with joy, for she had found our poor children and had given them the grapes.

"At another time, my aunt gave us some delicious figs which could arouse the most jaded appetite. Jacinta joyfully sat down with us by the side of the basket. She took the first one to eat it, but suddenly remembered something and said, 'It's true. Today we have not yet made any sacrifice for sinners. We've got to make this one.' Offering the sacrifice to God she placed the fig back in the basket, and we promptly followed her example. Jacinta repeated these sacrifices frequently, but I will not tell any more, else I shall never come to the end.

"One day in August the Blessed Virgin again recommended the practise of mortification, saying, 'Pray. Pray constantly, and make sacrifices, for many souls go to hell because there are none to mortify themselves and to pray for them.'

"A few days later, as we walked along the road with our flocks, I found a piece of rope. Picking it up, I playfully tied it to my arm. Before long I noticed that the rope was bruising me, and so I said to my cousins, 'Look, this hurts. We could tie it around our waists, and offer to God a little sacrifice.'

"The children accepted my idea, and we immediately divided the rope among the three of us, using the edge of a stone for a knife. The rope made us suffer horribly either because of its thickness or roughness, or because we tightened it too much. Now and then Jacinta wept for the pain, so I told her to remove it. But she answered, 'No, I want to offer this sacrifice to Our Lord in reparation and for the conversion of sinners.'

"On another day while we amused ourselves by plucking from the walls certain herbs which, when pressed in the hands, crack with a little noise, Jacinta unwittingly pricked her hands with some nettles. As she felt the pain, she squeezed them more in her hands and said, 'Look! Here is something else with which to mortify ourselves.'

"From that time on we used once in a while to beat our legs with the nettles, to offer God another sacrifice, and, if I am not mistaken, it was also during this month that we acquired the habit of giving our lunch to the poor."

The parents of the seers had been notified to appear with their children in the office of the Administrator. This they did. Lúcia was taken by her father but Jacinta's father did not go. Lúcia parted from Jacinta, who went with her brother to the well to pray. Lúcia tells us:

"At night when I returned, I went to the well and found the two kneeling there with their elbows on the edge and with their heads between their hands, weeping. They were surprised to see me and cried, 'Is it really you? Your sister came over here for water and told us that they had killed you. We have already prayed and cried for you very much.'

"Some time later, when we were in prison, her parents' neglect was the hardest thing for Jacinta to bear. With tears in her eyes she would say, 'Neither your parents nor mine have come to see us. They do not care for us any more.'

"But Francisco answered, 'Don't cry; rather offer this to Jesus for sinners.' Raising his eyes and hands to heaven, he himself made the offering, 'O my Jesus, it is for Your love and for the conversion of sinners.'

"Then Jacinta added, 'And also for the Holy Father and in reparation for the sins committed against the Immaculate Heart of Mary.'

"Later, after we had been separated, they brought us together into a room of the jail and said that in a little while they were going to fry us. Jacinta withdrew to the window, which looked out on the cattle market, and though at first I thought she was trying to distract herself with the view, I soon realized that she was weeping. I called her to me and asked why she cried.

"Amid her sobs she answered, 'Because we are going to die without seeing our parents again.'" And with tears running down her cheeks, she added, 'I would like to see my mother, at least.'

"'Don't you want to offer this sacrifice for the conversion of sinners?' I asked.

"'I do.' And at that, she lifted her hands and eyes to heaven and made the offering: 'O my Jesus, it is for Your love, for the conversion of sinners, for the Holy Father, and in reparation for the sins committed against the Immaculate Heart of Mary.'"

What the life of Jacinta was after the apparitions can be well summarized in these words which Lúcia wrote after a visit to her cousin in the hospital of Vila Nova de Ourém:

"I found her suffering joyfully for the love of our good God, of the Immaculate Heart of Mary, for sinners, and for the Holy Father. It was her ideal of which she never tired of speaking."

"She thought of nothing else; it was her dominating thought, a divine obsession.

"Ever since Our Lady taught us to offer our sacrifices, whenever we agreed to make any, or had some trial to undergo, Jacinta would ask: 'Have you told Jesus that it is for His love?'

"If I answered in the negative she would say, 'Then I will tell Him.' Whereupon she clasped her hands, raised her eyes to heaven and said, 'O

Jesus, it is for Your love and for the conversion of sinners.'"

Even the delights of the life of piety she sacrificed to the noble ambition of converting sinners. "Jacinta liked to visit the Blessed Sacrament during recreation in school. 'But,' she said, 'it seems that they guess our plans, for as soon as we go into the church there are so many people asking us questions. I would love to stay a long time alone with Our Lord, talking to the *hidden Jesus*,[4] but they never let us alone.'

"In fact, the simple people of the village never did let us alone. With all their simplicity they spoke to us about their troubles. To all Jacinta showed sympathy, but especially when it was a question of a sinner she would remark, 'We have to pray and offer sacrifices to Our Lord for his conversion, so that he may not go to hell, poor soul.'"

She suffered everything for the conversion of sinners, everything was sweet to her and seemed as nothing. One of the hardest things she had to endure was to answer the numerous questions people asked, but she could suffer that

---

4 Jesus escondido.

too. Whenever she escaped these, she substituted other sacrifices.

"To avoid those who sought her," writes Lúcia, "she hid with her little brother in a cave dug into a cliff on the east slope of the windmill-crowned mountain which faces our village. This cave afforded them excellent protection from the rain and from the heat of the sun, especially because it is sheltered by many olive and oak trees. How many prayers and sacrifices she offered there to our dear Lord, He alone knows."

Lúcia suffered no less than her companions but that, too, increased Jacinta's own suffering. Lúcia writes:

"At times Jacinta and Francisco found me in great affliction because of the attitude of my family, and since my voice was so choked with sobbing that I could hardly speak, they too, weeping bitterly, suffered with me. Jacinta then in a loud and clear voice would make the offering, 'My God, it is in reparation and for the conversion of sinners that we offer Thee all these sufferings and sacrifices.' (The formula was not always in the same words)."

So much suffering began to undermine Jacinta's health. This was to be expected. Not even an adult could stand such a struggle with the family, with the Administrator, and with herself. To top it all, her brother died. This piercing grief, however, was eased by the christian and supernatural manner in which he met death. Lúcia continues:

"When the moment arrived for her brother to go to heaven, she made her recommendation, 'Give my love to Our Lord and to Our Lady, and tell them that I suffer all they ask of me to convert sinners, and in reparation to the Immaculate Heart of Mary.'"

"All . . ." Generous souls know neither reserve nor limit in the way they give themselves to God. Love is paid only with love. Love consists in giving delight to the one loved, in doing his will, in realizing his desires—love is the union of hearts and wills. The love of God is manifested to souls in the suffering He sends them, for "God tries those whom He loves," and the love of souls for God consists in suffering with Him and for Him. Jacinta loved much; she was a model of atoning love. Sacrifices, persecutions, illness, death—everything was borne with love. This total and absolute giving is the foundation and crown of holiness. When made consciously, it represents complete detachment from creatures and perfect giving to God.

Jacinta voluntarily cut the ties of natural sympathy which bound her to creatures; she took the most difficult steps in the life of perfection, and securely made her way to the lofty heights of holiness.

The Secret
of the Lady

Anyone who has been interested in the apparitions of Fatima from the beginning has felt a curiosity and burning desire to uncover or see uncovered the mysterious secret which the children claimed to have received from the Lady, and which they kept inviolate in the face of the most alluring promises as well as the most terrifying threats. All three affirmed it, and all three kept it. Neither inquisitorial ability nor blandishments, neither the ecclesiastical authority of the pastor nor the civil authority of the Administrator achieved anything. The children were imprisoned, threatened with martyrdom, but all to no avail. The pastor was scandalized at their strange silence. Even the authority of His Excellency the Bishop of

Leiria was unduly invoked and that of the Provincial of the religious congregation of nuns to which Sister Maria Lúcia belonged—it was a titanic battle within the intimacy of the soul—but still to no avail. The secret was kept. Victorious over cunning and astuteness, it was kept—until now.

Precisely on this 25th anniversary of the apparitions[5] God has permitted the secret to be revealed, a secret which has held many souls in suspense, tormented with the idea of punishment which they imagine will inevitably fall upon us and upon our beloved Portugal. Let us thank Divine Providence for the revelation of the heavenly secret, and let us profit by the painful and serious yet healthy and regenerating teaching of this revelation concerning a doctrine which so many in our time have felt repugnance in accepting. Faith has not been strengthened, for it rests on the eternal word of Our Lord in Divine Revelation contained in the pages of Holy Scripture and in the Tradition of the Church, the pillar and foundation of truth. The same today as yesterday, the same always, since truth never changes, never compromises itself, never yields. However, we must rec-

---

5 The Portuguese edition was published originally in 1942.

ognize that such a vision offered to three innocent children in a place sanctified by the presence of the Mother of God assumes the aspect of a solemn warning to a generation drunk with pleasure and debased by the worship of material things.

The vision, the secret of which has been kept inviolate until today, took place on July 13, 1917, in the Cova da Iria. It was a vision of hell. Sister Maria Lúcia tells us about it:

"The secret consists in three distinct things, two of which I am going to reveal. The first was the vision of hell. Our Lord showed us a vast ocean of fire which seemed to lie underneath the earth. Submerged in that fire, like bronzed or blackened embers, transparent and glowing in human form, were the souls of the damned, hovering about, in and above the conflagration, driven back and forth by the flames which with great clouds of smoke issued from themselves, rising and falling on all sides like sparks in a great fire, without weight or balance, while from the midst of the pit arose frightful groans with terrifying shrieks of pain and of despair. The devils had horrible and foul forms of strange, fearsome animals, but they too, were transparent and black. This sight lasted only a moment, thanks to our good Mother, who had forearmed us in the first vision with the promise of taking us to heaven. If it were not for this, I believe we would have died of fear and terror."

Even some pious people refuse to speak to their children about hell, lest it frighten them, but God did not hesitate to show it to three children, one of whom was only six years old, and who He knew would be so horrified as almost to wither with fear.

"Frequently Jacinta sat on the ground or on a rock, and thoughtfully would say, 'To think of hell![6] How sorry I am for the souls who go to hell! Those people, burning there alive, like wood in a fire.'

"And trembling, she would kneel on the ground, clasping her hands, and say the prayer Our Lady had taught us:

"'Oh, my Jesus, forgive us our sins; save us from the fire of hell. Take all souls to heaven, especially those in greatest need.'

"She would remain like this for a long time, repeating the same prayer. Now and again, as though awakening from a dream, she would call me or Francisco:

---

6 *"O inferno! O inferno!"*

"Francisco, Francisco, are you two praying with me? It is necessary to pray much to save souls from hell. So many go there!'

"At other times, she would ask, 'Why does not Our Lady show hell to sinners? If they saw it, they would not sin, to avoid going there. Tell the Lady to show hell to all those people [she referred to the people who were at the Cova da Iria at the time of the apparition], and you will see how they will be converted!'

"After the apparition, somewhat unsatisfied, she asked me, 'Why didn't you tell Our Lady to show hell to those people?'

"'I forgot.'

"'I did not remember either,' she said sadly.

"But the vision of hell obsessed her, and she would ask anxiously again and again, 'What are the sins those people commit to go to hell?'

"'I do not know,' I would respond. 'Perhaps the sins of not going to Mass on Sunday, of stealing, of saying ugly words, of cursing, of swearing.'

"'And only for a simple word do they go to hell?'

"'Well, it's a sin.'"[7]

---

7 Lúcia, of course, means that these sins condemn to Hell only if they are serious enough to constitute mortal sins—as to miss Mass deliberately without sufficient reason, to steal a large amount, etc.

"'It wouldn't be hard for them to have been silent or to have gone to Mass, would it? I am so sorry for poor sinners. If only I could show hell to them!'

"Also she would suddenly get hold of me and say, 'I'm going to heaven, but you are staying here. If Our Lady lets you, tell everybody what hell is like, so that they will not commit any more sins, and will not go there. So many people falling into hell! So many people in hell!'

"'Don't be afraid. You are going to heaven.'

"'True. But I want all those people to go to heaven, too.'

"When, to mortify herself, she would refuse to eat, I would say, 'Come, Jacinta, eat something now.'

"'No,' she would reply, 'I want to offer this sacrifice for sinners who eat too much.'"

During Jacinta's illness, when Lúcia went to Mass on weekdays, she would say to her, "Jacinta, don't come. You can't—today is not Sunday."

Jacinta would answer immediately, "It doesn't matter. I want to go for sinners who do not go even on Sunday."

Whenever she heard an ugly word, she covered her face with her hands and said, "Oh, my

God, don't these people really know that they can go to hell for saying those things? Forgive them, my Jesus, and convert them. They certainly don't know that they offend God. What a pity, my Jesus! I pray for them." And then she would repeat the prayer taught by Our Lady, "Oh, my Jesus, forgive them. . . ."

This is the secret of the mortified life which Jacinta and her companions led. The vision of hell had horrified her to such an extent that all penances and mortifications seemed as nothing if they could save some souls from it. That vision of hell, and the memory of the torments of the damned in that abode of sorrow and pain, gave her in her suffering such a heroic courage that it frightens our softened generation. The horror provoked by the vision of hell, and the salutary effect produced in the soul of the seers, is no more than a repetition of what has taken place in the lives of some saints. For example, one day Our Lord showed to Saint Teresa of Jesus, the great reformer of the Carmelites, the place which had been reserved for her in hell had she not corresponded to a certain grace.

If that vision is so salutary, if because of it so many souls are transformed, why does not God do as Jacinta wished? Why does He not show it to everybody so that they might escape it? The answer has already been given by the Divine Master through the mouth of Abraham in the parable of Lazarus and the rich man.

"There was a certain rich man, who was clothed in purple and fine linen, and feasted sumptuously every day. And there was a certain beggar, named Lazarus, who lay at his gate, full of sores, desiring to be filled with the crumbs that fell from the rich man's table, and no one did give him; moreover, the dogs came, and licked his sores.

"And it came to pass that the beggar died, and was carried by the angels into Abraham's bosom. And the rich man also died: and he was buried in hell. And lifting up his eyes when he was in torments, he saw Abraham afar off, and Lazarus in his bosom.

"And he cried and said: Father Abraham, have mercy on me, and send Lazarus, that he may dip the tip of his finger in water, to cool my tongue: for I am tormented in this flame.

"And Abraham said to him: Son, remember that thou didst receive good things in thy lifetime, and likewise Lazarus evil things: but now he is comforted: and thou art tormented. And besides all this, between us and you, there is fixed a great chaos: so that they who would pass from hence to you, cannot, nor from thence come hither.

"And he said: Then, father, I beseech thee, that thou wouldst send him to my father's house, for I have five brethren, that he may testify unto them, lest they also come into this place of torments.

"And Abraham said to him: They have Moses and the prophets; let them hear them. But he said: No, father Abraham; but if one went to them from the dead, they will do penance. And he said to him: If they hear not Moses and the prophets, neither will they believe, if one rise again from the dead." (*Luke* 16: 19–31).

It is the mission of the Church, which she fulfills without failing, to announce to the world eternal truths. Let the world listen. She is the heir of her Immaculate Spouse, Christ Jesus, of Whom the Eternal Father said on the height of Tabor, "This is my beloved Son, in Whom I am well pleased. Hear you Him." To hear the voice of the Holy Catholic Church, outside of which there is no salvation, is to listen to Christ Himself. And for those whose steps have strayed from the narrow path, here is a friendly counsel. Do not fail to take part in one of those spiritual retreats which today are going on almost continuously, such as

have been held now for many years at the Shrine
of Our Lady of Fatima, for men and women, boys
and girls, priests, doctors, lawyers, laborers, students, members of Catholic Action—for people of
all classes and conditions. Only God knows how
many souls have turned resolutely to Him after
meditating silently on hell, in the midst of tears
of confusion and remorse, and under the maternal smile of Mary in the delightful and unforgettable hours of that heavenly light—the spiritual
retreat—a work to which the Bishop of Leiria with
almost prophetic foresight has devoted the best of
his apostolic care as shepherd of souls.

Fountain
of Light

The second part of the secret entrusted to the children was the request for the establishment of the devotion to the Immaculate Heart of Mary.[8] On June 13, 1917, Our Lady reassured Lúcia that she would never abandon her, that her Immaculate Heart would be her refuge and the way that would lead her to God.

"As she said these words, she opened her hands and caused the light which came out from them to penetrate our hearts. It seems to me that

---

8 On October 31, 1942, the Holy Father, Pius XII, consecrated the whole Church to the Immaculate Heart of Mary, on the occasion of the 25th Anniversary of the Apparitions at Fatima. In 1945, the Feast of the Immaculate Heart of Mary was extended by the same Pontiff to the Universal Church, and its celebration set for August 22nd.

on that day this light had as its chief end to infuse in us a special knowledge and love of the Immaculate Heart of Mary. From that day on we felt in our hearts a more burning love for it.

"Jacinta would tell me now and again, 'The Lady said that her Immaculate Heart would be your refuge and the way to lead you to God. Don't you love it? I love her heart so much! It is so good!'

"I have already told how Jacinta chose from the litany of ejaculations which Father Cruz[9] suggested to us the one which says, 'Sweet Heart of Mary, be my salvation.' After reciting it, she would add with that simplicity which was so natural to her: 'I love the Immaculate Heart of Mary so much! It is the heart of our good Mother in heaven. Don't you love to say many times, "Sweet Heart of Mary, Immaculate Heart of Mary"? I love it so much, so very much!'

"As she picked flowers from the field she would sing two melodies improvised by herself, 'Sweet Heart of Mary, be my salvation! Immaculate Heart of Mary, convert sinners, save souls from hell.'"

---

9 A very old priest, widely known in Portugal for his holiness, who befriended the children in their hour of need.

Up to now they were given only promises
and inducements. But July 13 marked a step for-
ward. It was no longer a question of promises or of
vague requests. After the vision of hell, the Lady
continued to speak to them and told them what
she wanted and under what conditions. The sequel
was tragic. In due time, Sister Maria Lúcia made
repeated attempts before the proper authorities
to carry out the Lady's wishes. In a letter of June,
1938, to the Bishop of Leiria, she made a clear reference to the approaching war. "Now that these
things are so close at hand. . . ."—and she declared
to us orally that she would reveal part of the secret
"if the Bishop so ordered." This is the way Sister
Maria Lúcia describes the second part of the vision
of July 13:

"We next lifted our eyes to Our Lady, who
told us with kindness and sadness:

"'You have seen hell, where the souls of poor
sinners go. To save them, God wishes to establish in
the world the devotion to my Immaculate Heart.
If they do what I am going to tell you, many souls
will be saved and there will be peace. This war is
going to end, but if men do not stop offending
God, in the reign of the next Pontiff a worse war
will start. When you see the night illumined by an

unknown light, know that it is the great sign that God gives you[10] that He is about to punish the world for its crimes by means of war, of hunger, and of persecutions of the Church and the Holy Father. To forestall this, I will come to request the consecration of Russia to my Immaculate Heart, and communion in reparation on every first Saturday. If they heed my request, Russia will be converted and there will be peace; if not, its errors will be spread throughout the world, promoting wars and persecutions of the Church. The good will be martyred, the Holy Father will have much to suffer, various nations will be annihilated, but in the end my Immaculate Heart will triumph. The Holy Father will consecrate Russia to me, and it will be converted, and some time of peace will be granted to the world.'"

Even though the outstanding apostle of the devotion to the Immaculate Heart of Mary, in the designs of Providence, is Sister Maria Lúcia (and such is the opinion of Jacinta in the words that follow), our little heroine herself is far from being a stranger to that enterprise. Was there anything noble, beautiful, or sublime at Fatima

---

10 The sign would be for them and not necessarily for the whole world.

which did not make her soul vibrate with love and enthusiasm? This is how her cousin Lúcia, after so many little details scattered throughout the book, describes the attitude of Jacinta toward this devotion:

"Shortly before going to the hospital, Jacinta told me:

"'It will not be long now before I go to heaven. You stay behind, make known that God wants to establish in the world the devotion to the Immaculate Heart of Mary. Whenever you will speak of this, do not hesitate, but tell everybody that God grants us graces through the Immaculate Heart of Mary, that they should ask her for them, that the Heart of Jesus wants the Immaculate Heart of Mary to be venerated with His own. Tell them that they should ask for peace, that God has granted it to her. Oh, if I could only kindle in everybody's heart the fire which I have here in my breast burning me and making me love the Heart of Jesus and the Heart of Mary so much!'

"One day someone gave me a picture of the Heart of Jesus, rather beautiful for what man can do. I took it to Jacinta.

"'Do you want this Holy Picture?' I asked her.

"She took it, looked at it with attention, and said, 'It is so ugly! It doesn't look at all like Our Lord, Who is so beautiful. But I would like to keep it. After all, it is still He.'

"And she carried it with her all the time. At night, and all during her illness, she kept it under her pillow until the picture was torn. She would kiss it frequently and say, 'I kiss His Heart because I like it best. I wish I had also the Heart of Mary. Don't you have one? I would like to have the two together.'"

Like Baltassar in the sacrilegious orgy of Babylon, and still today as always, in spite of these warnings from heaven many impious people will continue to laugh, carelessly to make merry, and foolishly to neglect the most important business—the salvation of their own souls. How greedily they drain the cup of pleasures! We like to repeat the word of the Divine Saviour over the city of Jerusalem: "If thou also hadst known, and that in this thy day, the things that are to thy peace!" (*Luke* 19, 42). Let us remember that God, does not desire "the death of the wicked, but that the wicked turn from his way, and live." (Ezech. 33:11.) But for this to happen, it is indispensable that the "impious abandon his perverse ways," and turn to God, "the fountain of living water" (*Jer.* 2:13). May a tender devotion to the Immaculate Heart of Mary, to whom our venerable bishops have consecrated at Fatima the Portuguese people, be the beginning and the sure pledge of national salvation!

Unto Death

The official persecution was now beginning. Vila Nova de Ourém, the Prefecture to which Fatima belongs, was and is profoundly Catholic, but for various reasons, following the establishment of the new regime in 1910, authority was for a long time in the hands of a shameless and bold individual who, as head of a Masonic "triangle," and of the "democratic" party, was practically the master of the district. When news of the apparitions began to spread, he watched closely to see what would happen. Brazen Jacobin that he was, the "Tinsmith" (as he was called), at that time Administrator of the district, decided to agitate what he termed a reactionary manifestation.

The people of the villages trembled at the very thought of being called to the Administration. It can be well imagined, therefore, what an impression was made on the souls of the three little shepherds and their families when they were notified to appear at the "Tinsmith's" office. This is how Lúcia narrates the incident:

"Not many days after, my uncle and my parents received orders from the authorities to appear at the Administration the following day, at a fixed hour—my uncle with Jacinta and Francisco, and my father with me. The Administration is at Vila Nova de Ourém, and for that reason we had to walk about three leagues, a very considerable distance for children of our age. The only means of traveling at that time and in that region were on foot or by donkey.

"My uncle replied immediately that he would go but that he was not taking his children with him. 'On foot they will never make it, and riding they will never hold themselves on the donkey because they are not used to it. Moreover, there is no reason for taking two children of their age to court.'

"My father thought otherwise: 'My girl is going: let her answer for herself; as for me I understand nothing of these things; if she lies it is proper that she be punished.'

"On the following day, early in the morning, they sat me on the donkey, from which I fell three times on the way.

"Then it was that the family took occasion to frighten us in every possible way. Before leaving Fatima, as we passed in front of my uncle's house, my father waited a few minutes for him. I ran to Jacinta's bed to say good-by to her.

"When she saw me in so great affliction, the poor child began to cry and said: 'If they kill you, tell them that Francisco and I are just like you and want to die too.'

"It cannot be imagined how much Jacinta and Francisco suffered on that day, thinking that the authorities were going to kill me. What caused me the greatest suffering was my parents' indifference toward me. At the Administration I was questioned by the Administrator in the presence of my father, my uncle, and several gentlemen I did not know. The Administrator insisted that I reveal the secret, and that I promise him never to return to Cova da Iria. To achieve his purpose he did not spare promises and timely threats. Seeing that it was all of no avail, he dismissed me, protesting that he would win out even if he had to kill me for it. He reprimanded my uncle severely for not having complied with his orders, and then let us go.

"One day three gentlemen came to speak to us. After their questioning, in which I had found no pleasure, they departed saying: 'See to it that you decide to reveal that secret, otherwise the Administrator is prepared to put an end to your lives.'

"Jacinta's face brightened with joy. 'O good, how wonderful! she exclaimed. 'I love Our Lord and Our Lady very much, and in this way we are going to see them very soon.'

"When the rumor went abroad that the Administrator really wanted to kill us, one of my aunts who lived at Casais came to our house with the intention of taking us away to her own. She lived in another district where the Administrator could not interfere with our safety. But her intention was not realized, for we refused to go, answering, 'If they kill us, it is all the same. We are going to heaven.'

"In the meantime the 13th of August dawned. Since the evening before, people had been arriving from every quarter. Everybody wanted to see us, to question us, to present requests through us to the Blessed Virgin. In the hands of those people we were like a ball in the hands of boys: everyone pulled us to his side and asked us his questions without allowing us time to answer anybody. In the midst of this uproar there fell an order from the Administrator, telling me to go to my aunt's house where he was waiting for me. My father was notified of this and so he took me there.

"When I arrived, the Administrator was in the room with my cousins. There he interrogated us and made new attempts to force us to reveal the secret and to promise not to return to Cova da Iria. His tactics failing, he ordered my father and my uncle to take us to the house of the parish priest where he submitted us to a new questioning."

Neither questions nor promises, not even threats, achieved anything. Then through the mind of the Administrator crossed the idea of carrying out the plan minutely elaborated by him and by his advisers, but which he had kept absolutely secret, lest anyone should discover it and lead the people to defend the children. He had resolved to take them prisoners to Vila Nova de Ourém. Pretending that he was going to Cova da Iria, he offered to take the children in his car, saying that thus they would arrive sooner at the place of the apparitions.

"My father," writes Lúcia, "said that he would walk, but the Administrator insisted that it was better for us to go by car, since we would not be harrassed by the people. Then, at my father's bidding, I climbed into the car with my cousins. The driver turned to the right and headed toward Vila Nova de Ourém. 'It is not this way!', I said, but the Administrator answered that he was going to Ourém to see the parish priest, and that we would be back on time. What hurt me as well as my cousins most at this time was the complete abandonment by the family.

"When we arrived at Ourém, they locked us in a room, and told us that we would not get out of it until we revealed the secret. Later they took us to the Administration where we were questioned anew, and gold pieces were offered to us as a bribe to reveal the secret. We returned to the house of the Administrator, and in the afternoon we were again questioned on the secret.

"Then they took us to jail and promised to leave us there if we did not reveal the secret. They threatened to fry us in boiling oil. The Administrator asked us to withdraw, and told a man to prepare a cauldron with boiling oil. Then he called Jacinta, saying that she was to be the first to be fried. She went readily and without saying goodbye. After questioning her, they put her in a room. Next they called Francisco. He was told that Jacinta was already fried, and that he was going to meet the same fate if he did not reveal the secret. They also questioned him, and then sent him to the same room. My turn came next. They told me that my cousins had already been burned, and that I could expect the same fate unless I told the secret. Even though I believed what they said was true, I was not afraid. They sent me to my cousins, but a man told us that it would not be long before the three of us would be fried.

"Later they took us to the Administrator's house, and there we stayed all night in the same room. The following day brought little change to the situation: questionings in the morning and in the afternoon accompanied by many threats and promises. On the next day, at ten o'clock, we went once again to the Administration, but as at previous times they could get nowhere with us. Then the Administrator ordered us to climb into a car and took us to the veranda of the parish priest's house, where he left us."

The fear of the children at this time, and how much they must have suffered, can well be imagined. They were very little. Lúcia was ten, and Jacinta was less than seven. Timid and shy, they had to face strange people who looked anything but friendly. Those must have been horrible days. They were thoroughly convinced that they were going to die. Jacinta wept with grief; Lúcia tried to comfort her. The prisoners advised them to reveal the secret, but they rejected the advice. They said the rosary before a medal belonging to Jacinta which a prisoner had hung from a nail on the wall. The prisoners themselves knelt and followed them. At the end of the rosary, Jacinta went to the window to cry.

Asked by her cousin whether she wanted to suffer for sinners, she answered, "I do, but I think of my mother and cannot help crying."

Seeing that he could do nothing with them, the Administrator took them to the parish priest. (He feared to return to Fatima through the narrow mountain roads.)

Our Lady did not fail to reward our little heroes. As they watched their flock at Valinhos—between Aljustrel and the Cabeço—on the 16th, she appeared to them on a holm oak, by the roadside in a place marked by a heap of stones.

Yet the persecution did not end here. In October, after the apparitions had ceased, enraged Masonry ordered a new feat of prowess.

"In the meanwhile," writes Lúcia, "the government was not satisfied with the turn events had taken. There had been set up in the place of the apparitions a few planks in the shape of an arch from which hung a few lanterns kept burning by the devotion of the people. One night the Administrator sent a man in an automobile to knock down these planks, to cut down the oak tree on which Our Lady had stood, and to drag it after the automobile. In the morning news of the vandalism spread rapidly. I ran over there to see if it were true, but what was my joy when I saw that the poor man had made a mistake and that instead of the oak (of which only the trunk worn down to the ground now stood), they had taken one of the nearby trees. Then and there I asked Our Lady to forgive those poor men and I prayed for their conversion."

Personal doubts, the indifference of the clergy, the attitude of the family and of the parish priest, and the official persecution surrounding the fact

of the apparitions at Fatima, these are all characteristic signs of the things of God. The persecution
made manifest the courage of the three little shepherds. It could be said even then, with the people
who gathered in multitudes, "Here indeed is the
finger of God!"

The Little Apostle

The fruits of Jacinta's generous cooperation with the grace of God are being manifested to us only now. In this chapter we shall attempt to summarize her apostolate following the transformation which took place under the influence of the apparitions. Today, when it has become so necessary for all of us to work for the salvation of our brethren, but there is still so much misunderstanding, so much apathy and lack of good will, may the example and personality of the little apostle Jacinta Marto strengthen and encourage those engaged in the front lines of the apostolate. It may even convert and awaken certain lethargic souls. The love of God is unique in this: the more intense it is, the more does it wish to communicate itself. Its only desire is to see Love more and more loved by all creatures. The saints pine away with love. Filled with grief, Saint Francis of Assisi roamed through the forests exclaiming, "Love is not loved, Love is not loved!" The life of Jacinta was a growing absorption in God, with Whom she became enamored, and for Whose glory she sacrificed herself.

Only a person who likes to dance knows what a sacrifice it is suddenly to forego this entertainment. Lúcia tells us that the shepherds on the mountain and the children of her age gave up dancing because the three little friends decided to give it up. Jacinta was the one who loved to dance. She could dance more artistically than the other two. Sister Maria de Jesus writes:

"Around the Feast of Saint John (after the second apparition, that of July 13th), she told me: 'Now I am not going to dance any more.'

"'Why?'

"'Because I want to offer this sacrifice to Our Lord.'

"And because we were the leaders in the games among the children, our example put an end to the dances which ordinarily were held on this occasion."

Even then, Jacinta was the forerunner of a heroic and hidden (even if not unknown) spirit of sacrifice in renouncing an entertainment in which many of them saw no evil. May God bless and multiply such heroism!

In their eagerness to play, Jacinta and her two companions had been saying the rosary badly, merely pronouncing the first words of the Hail Mary and of the Our Father. Perhaps even on the day of the first apparition, the rosary had been said in that way. After the apparitions, she was the one who immediately reminded the others of the obligation henceforth to say it well. Many times the thought of saying the rosary and the necessity of sacrifice, the mainspring of her new life, cut into her conversation and play. She knew well that it was only a dangerous illusion to want to do the work of her apostolate without prayer and sacrifice.

At home, even with her parents, she was never shy in the exercise of her apostolate. There she began the work of her conquest for Christ and of the perfection of her soul. In spite of all that has been said in praise of the Christian life and of the spirit of piety of the two families, the truth remains that not all should be taken literally. Not everything in them was perfect and worthy of imitation. Far from it. The grace of the apparitions was not a reward of virtue and piety, but a free gift which our beloved country was to enjoy much more than the seers themselves or their families. Lúcia's father (may God rest him!) was many years without making his Easter duty, and his life was hardly edifying. In Jacinta's own family many days went by without the recitation of the rosary. Understanding that the first field of our apostolate of Catholic Action must be the family, Jacinta did not rest until she brought her own family to a daily recitation of the rosary in common. It was a joy to watch her approach her mother, tenderly and sweetly, trying to convince her to be faithful to this devotion. Jacinta did not desist from her pleas until she was assured that they all would really say the rosary together.

The fervor of charity and zeal for the salvation of souls fired her life and led her to immolate herself as a little victim in union with the suffering of Jesus for the salvation of sinners. It moved her to do the work of the apostolate wherever she was. We have seen her in jail overcome by sorrow at the thought of not seeing her parents again. But even there when Lúcia simply reminded her of sinners, her tears dried in her eyes as if by magic.

"We decided then to say the rosary," Lúcia writes. "Jacinta took a medal which she wore around her neck, and asked one of the prisoners to hang it from a nail on the wall. Kneeling before the medal we began to pray. The prisoners prayed with us as best they knew. At least they knelt. When the rosary was over, Jacinta turned to the window and began to cry.

"'Jacinta, don't you want to offer this sacrifice to Our Lord?' I asked her.

"'Yes, but when I think of my mother, I cannot help crying.'

"Then, since the Blessed Virgin had told us to offer our prayers and sacrifices also in reparation for sins committed against her Immaculate Heart, we agreed among ourselves that each one of us should offer them for a different intention, one for sinners, one for the Holy Father, and one in reparation for the sins committed against the Immaculate Heart of Mary. When the agreement was made, I told Jacinta to choose the intention she liked.

"'I offer mine for all the intentions, for I like them all,' she said."

As the end approached, Jacinta noticed how little attention the people paid to the recommendations of Our Lady. She was grieved, and once in a while she revealed her anguish to her two companions. Once, during her illness, she turned to Lúcia and said:

"Don't you know Our Lord is sad? Our Lady told us that people should not offend Him any more because He is already much offended. But nobody listens. They go on committing the same sins."

She fell ill, but not even in the hospital did her work for souls slacken. Like the lamp which before it goes out for want of oil, lets out a last glimmer and only then is extinguished, so it was with Jacinta, when she felt that life was departing, and that only a little time remained for her work. She intensified the love and zeal which consumed her. In those last days, in order to make the most of the flickers of life which were left to her, she prayed, counseled, censured, and only then did she peacefully sleep in the Lord.

The immodest dress of some nurses, and the behavior of a few doctors, whom she supposed to be unbelieving, led her to remind them of eternity, and to ask them to avoid "luxury and immodest dress." New revelations of Our Lady made her exclaim, "Oh, I am so sorry for Our Lady, I am so

sorry!" And like the echo of the voice of the Blessed
Virgin, she said solemnly that the sin which leads
most people to perdition is the sin of impurity;
that people must not grow hardened in sin, and
that it is necessary to do much penance.

Always and everywhere Jacinta was a living example of virtue in action, conquering
the souls of children and adults alike. Even before
she entered the hospital, while living with a char-
itable person who had received her in her home,
Jacinta did not lose an opportunity to do good,
or to lead others to do better. To another little girl
who lived in the same house, Jacinta recommended
many times, "Be very obedient, never be lazy, and
never tell a lie."

From the official questioning of Senhora
Maria da Purificação Godinho, made in the College of Our Lady of Fatima, on September 11,
1934, we extract the following information concerning Jacinta's life during these last days:

"She did not play, ate little, did not complain
about her illness; she said the rosary every day, did
not like to hear lies, reprimanded persons who told
them in her presence, and showed always a great
love for truth. She asked this lady whenever she
went to church to warn the persons whom she saw

talking there. In case they did not receive her well and insulted her, she was to suffer all patiently for the love of Our Lord.

"When she prayed from the balcony which looked into the Chapel of Our Lady of Miracles, she liked to be in a place where she could see the tabernacle. As she prayed thus, her attitude and the expression on her face, with her eyes fervently fixed on the tabernacle, made an impressive sight. While she was still at home in Aljustrel but already very sick, her cousin brought her a holy card with the chalice and host on it. She took it, kissed it fervently, and radiant with joy, as though wrapt in a beautiful dream or in a far-off vision, she told her, 'It is the Hidden Jesus. I love Him very much. I wish I could receive Him in church. . . . Do you receive Communion in heaven? If they do, I am going to receive every day. I wish the angel would give me Communion again at the hospital. How happy I would be!'

"Sometimes as I returned from church and entered her house, she would ask me, 'Did you receive?'

"If I said yes, she added immediately, 'Come very close to me, because you have in your heart the Hidden Jesus.'

"At other times, she would tell me, 'I don't know how it is. I feel Our Lord inside of me, I understand what He tells me, but I do not see or hear Him. But it is so good to be with Him.'

"At six o'clock in the afternoon of Friday, the 20th of February, Jacinta said she felt very ill, that she wished to receive the sacraments. The pastor of the parish was called. He heard her confession about eight o'clock that evening. They told me that the little girl insisted that the Holy Viaticum be brought to her, but the pastor refused, since he thought that she looked well. However, he promised to bring Our Lord on the following day. The little girl persisted in asking for Holy Communion, saying that she would die shortly. In fact, at ten-thirty that evening, she died in the greatest tranquillity."

She passed away without having received Communion, except from the hands of the Angel during the apparition at the Cabeço. Jacinta never made her First Holy Communion, not even as Viaticum. Her father thinks she did, but the pastor and Sister Maria Lúcia, with whom we spoke, say that he has confused Jacinta with Teresa Marto, her sister, who was Lúcia's partner in their First Communion. This is not surprising. The prejudice

against giving Communion to very young children was still widespread. The precept of Pius X
in regard to frequent Communion was not being
fulfilled. Solemn Communion was given between
the ages of ten and twelve, and generally this
was the First Communion. The contrary was the
exception. Only God knows the suffering of that
little heart, enamored of the Eucharistic Jesus, and
kept far away from Him. I suppose that it was the
greatest immolation of little Jacinta. Through it
may we obtain the grace of seeing children receive
early, often, and fervently.

The Clergy and the Seers

Except for a very few priests who even in the press favored the persecution against Fatima, judging the whole affair to be superstitious, the majority of the clergy maintained a prudent reserve and waited. This was only fitting. After the apparitions there was an investigation of the case which the Reverend Pastor of Fatima officially reported to the Cardinal Patriarch, his hierarchical superior. Ordered to institute a process, he obeyed. Witnesses were summoned—the parents and their children, the seers themselves. He investigated everything, and at the end of the hearing he forwarded the process to the Patriarchal Curia. He wanted to see things clearly, but that grace was denied him; and because he did not see clearly, he remained unbelieving even after so many questionings.

But this was not the first case of the kind in the history of the Church. Various things seemed strange to him, one of which was the erection of a chapel in a deserted place far away from any center of population. The parish church was itself under repairs. He thought it more reasonable that alms should be brought to the parish to defray the heavy expenses of the construction, rather than that they be given for the erection of a chapel in the wilderness. For that reason, in his last questioning of Lúcia, he cross-examined her more strictly. She writes:

"The pastor also subjected me to his last questioning. The time appointed for the events had come to an end, and his Reverence, who did not know what to say about all this, began to show his displeasure.

"'Why are all those people going to prostrate themselves in prayer in a desert place, while the Living God, the God of our altars, God in the Blessed Sacrament is left alone, abandoned in the tabernacle? What is all that money for, left by them without any purpose under that holm-oak, while the church under repairs cannot be completed for lack of funds?' he asked.

"If I had been the master of the hearts of those people, I would certainly have led them to the parish church, but since I was not, I offered to God one more sacrifice. The good pastor continued to show himself more and more displeased and perplexed concerning the events, and one day left the parish. The news then was spread abroad that his Reverence had left the parish because of me, since he did not want to assume the responsibility that the facts imposed. He was a zealous pastor, much beloved of the people, and so I had much to suffer."

Several pious women, irritated by the loss which his departure had caused the parish, found Lúcia one day and insulted and beat her. Jacinta regretted that she could not suffer in like manner.

But it was not the pastor alone who observed and questioned the three children. Many others, especially priests, either from mere curiosity or from zeal, or even as a form of study, stopped to question them at length and in detail. Whenever they could, the children ran away from them. Jacinta remained only when she could not escape, and if she had to stay, she kept silence.

"Since Jacinta was accustomed to lower her head, fix her eyes on the ground, and say nothing during the interviews, I was almost always called upon to satisfy the curiosity of the pilgrims," writes Lúcia. "For that reason I was constantly being summoned to the house of the pastor to be interviewed by this or that other person, by this or that other priest. On one occasion a priest from Torres Novas came to see me. He asked for such minute details in a manner so filled with ruses that afterward I retained some scruples for having hidden some things from him. I consulted my cousins on the case.

"'I don't know,' I said to them, 'if we are doing wrong by not telling everything. When they ask us if Our Lady told us anything else, I do not know whether we lie or not when we say that she told us a secret but refuse to reveal the rest.'

"'I don't know, either,' answered Jacinta. 'You decide. You're the one who does not want us to say anything.'

"'Of course I don't want you to say anything,' I answered, 'they would then ask us what mortification we are making, and that would be the limit! Listen, if you had not said anything, nobody would know now that we had seen the Lady, spoken to her, or to the Angel. Besides, nobody had to know it.'

"A little while later, another priest from Santarem appeared. He looked like the brother of the first. As least, it seemed that they had rehearsed their parts together—the same questions, the same tricks and ruses, the same mannerisms in laughing and in scoffing. Even their stature and features seemed to be the same. After this interview, my doubt increased, and I really did not know what to do. I asked Our Lord and Our Lady constantly to tell me what to do.

"'O, my God, my Mother in Heaven, you know that I do not want to offend you with lies, but you see well that it is not fitting for me to say all that you told me.'

"One day we were told that a holy priest was coming to see us, one who could tell what was going on in the heart of everyone, and that he was to discover whether we told the truth or not. Full of joy, Jacinta exclaimed, 'When is that Father coming! If he guesses right, he will know very well that we are speaking the truth.'

"Another day, we were sitting a few steps away from Jacinta's house under the shade of the fig trees which spread out over the street. In

his play, Francisco withdrew away from us a bit.
Noticing that several ladies were approaching,
he ran to bring us the news. At that time ladies'
hats had brims almost as broad as a sieve, and we
thought that with such a thing on their heads,
they would never see us; so without further ado we
climbed one of the fig trees. As soon as the ladies
had passed by, we hurried down, and hastened to
hide in a cornfield. This habit of escaping whenever we could was part of the pastor's complaint.
His Reverence complained that we ran away from
everyone, especially priests. He spoke the truth,
but then it was especially priests who questioned
us again and again without mercy. Whenever we
found ourselves in the presence of a priest, we dis-
posed ourselves to offer to God one of our greatest
sacrifices."

The questionings were repeated over and over
again as if it were a police investigation. Eagerness
to know, curiosity, an itching desire to talk with the
seers, all these practically removed them from
the bosom of their families. In reference to the
afternoon of October 13, 1917, after the wonderful
happenings at the Cova da Iria, Lúcia writes:

"I spent the afternoon of that day with my
cousins. The multitudes tried to see and observe

us as though we were a curious monster of some sort. Night found me truly tired of so many questionings, which however did not come to an end with the night itself. Several persons who had been unable to question me remained for the following day, waiting for their turn. A few of them wanted to talk to me even at night but I was so overcome by fatigue that I dropped to the ground asleep.

"Thanks be to God, human respect and self-love at that time were still unknown to me. For that reason I was as much at ease with others as with my own parents. On the following day, or rather on the following days, the interviews continued. From that time on several persons went almost daily to the Cova da Iria to implore the protection of the Mother of God, and everybody wanted to look at the seers, ask their own questions, and say the rosary with them. At times I was so tired of repeating the same thing and also of praying, that I looked for any pretext to excuse myself and escape, but those poor people insisted so earnestly that I sometimes had to make an extreme effort in order to satisfy them."

However, God be thanked, their contact with priests was not limited to questionings and cross-examinations. There were priestly hearts, some still remembered, others already dimmed by the mists of time, who exercised to the utmost their sacerdotal mission in behalf of the three children. In spite of the suffering they had to undergo because of his unbelief, Lúcia and her cousins nurtured always a great love and respect for their pastor. There were other priests whose influence was more intense and more profound than his, probably due to the fact that it was free of the thorns which followed the influence of Father Ferreira.

One day a priest came to see Lúcia. He talked, examined, questioned. In the end, he counseled her and said: "You must love Our Lord very much for the many graces and favors which He is granting you."

"These words were so deeply engraved on my soul," she writes, "that since then I have acquired the habit of saying to Our Lord constantly: 'My God, I love you, in thanksgiving for the graces which You have granted to me.'

"I passed this ejaculation on to Jacinta and Francisco. She took it so much to heart that in the midst of her most absorbing games she would ask, 'Have you been forgetting to tell Our Lord that you love Him for the graces He has granted us?'

"One day it was the turn of the Reverend Dr. Cruz of Lisbon to interview us. After his questioning, he requested us to go with him to the place where Our Lady had appeared to us. On that day we walked on either side of his Reverence, who rode a donkey so short that the good Father almost dragged his feet on the ground. He taught us a litany of ejaculations, two of which Jacinta retained and which she never ceased repeating ever afterward: 'Oh my Jesus, I love you! Sweet Heart of Mary, be my salvation!'

"One day, during her illness, she told me, 'I love so much to tell Jesus that I love Him . . . Many times when I say it to Him it seems that I have a fire here inside of my breast, but it does not burn me.'

"At another time she said, 'I love Our Lord and Our Lady so much that I never get tired of telling them that I love them.'"

We bring this chapter to a close with the pleasant memory of a charming priestly personality who exercised a profound influence on the seers. God has already called him to Himself and for that reason we can, without the risk of wounding his modesty, speak openly of his virtues, of his zeal, and of his piety. He is the pastor of Olival and

Vicar of Forane of Ourém, the Reverend Father
Faustino José Jacinto Ferreira. The best proof of
his zeal consists in the fact that during the years
of his ministry at Olival no less than twenty-eight
priests ascended the steps of the altar—and it was
he who had led their first steps toward the sanctuary. Let us quote from the *Voz da Fatima* a few
remarks concerning this beloved Priest:

"Father Faustino, a distinguished figure of
former times, was as much at home and as full
of good will at the Court and at the Patriarchal
Palace, as in the humblest dwelling of his parish.
He had seen two generations arise, molded by his
apostolic labors, and many of the priests who then
ministered in the parishes of the Vicariate he had
directed toward the sanctuary.

"The clergy there formed a kind of family whose chief was Father Faustino, not merely
by disposition of the authorities, but rather by
choice of friendship, honor, and esteem. Everyone had the fullest confidence in him. Whatever
decision he made was reverently accepted by the
others, and his opinion was always received with
respect and love. For them he was the master, the
model, and the friend. One has only to recall
the gatherings of the clergy in his residence at

Olival to have the most unequivocal proof of this. That he was eminent among the parochial clergy is proved by the fact that he was chosen for the first group of Diocesan Consultors.

"Possessing an unusual memory and a keen intelligence, he knew each one of his almost 7,000 parishioners by name, and always had before him the various circumstances of their physical, moral, civil, and religious life. In him virtue excelled the gifts of nature. His well-known piety, his devotion to Our Lady and to the souls in purgatory, his zeal for the House of God and for the splendor of divine worship made of him the honor of his country and the idol of his people. It was for all these reasons that with the coming of the republic, and even later, the Jacobins of the region could find no better way of insulting the Catholic religion than by besmirching the venerable name of the pastor of Olival. They threw him in jail and kept him there for several hours."

Who could have imagined that between that venerable and venerated priest and the seers there existed a very intimate bond, and that his influence extended even to these humble souls, although they hardly belonged to his jurisdiction?

"In the midst of this perplexity," writes Sister Maria Lúcia, "I had the good fortune of speaking with the pastor of Olival. I do not know why but his Reverence inspired confidence in me and I revealed to him my doubt. It was he who taught us how to keep the secret. He gave us a few instructions on the spiritual life, and he especially taught us how to please Our Lord in everything, and how to offer Him a multitude of little sacrifices.

"'If you feel like eating some particular thing, my children,' he would say, 'let it go and in its place eat something else, and offer the sacrifice to God. If you feel like playing, do not do it and offer to God still another sacrifice. If people question you and you cannot escape them, it is God who wants it so—offer it to Him also as a sacrifice.'

"I really understood the admirable language of the venerable priest, and loved him dearly from then on. Father Faustino never again lost sight of my soul, and once in a while he would stop in to see me, or keep in touch with me through a pious woman, Senhora Emilia, who lived in a small hamlet near Olival (Soutaria). This woman went very often to the Cova da Iria to pray. She would then pass by our house and ask me to spend a few days at the house of Father Faustino. His Reverence was so kind as to ask me to stay in his residence for two or three days as company for his niece. It was at such times that he would patiently spend long hours with me, teaching me the practise of virtue and guiding me with his wise counsel. Even though I did not at the time understand anything about spiritual direction, I may nevertheless say that he was my first spiritual director. I cherish, therefore, grateful and holy memories of this venerable priest of God."

His influence was likewise felt by little Jacinta. How the soul of Father Faustino looked into the future! Lúcia refers to his paternal solicitude when she writes:

"One day when I had occasion to speak with Father, his Reverence asked me how Jacinta was. I told him what I thought about her health, and that she had revealed to me that she could not bend down to the ground to pray. He then told me to tell her not to get down from her bed again to pray, but that she should lie in bed and pray only as long as she could without getting tired.

"I gave her the message at the earliest opportunity and she asked me, 'Do you think Our Lord will be pleased?'

"'Yes,' I answered, 'Our Lord wants us to do what Father Faustino says.'

"'Then it is all right. I will never get up again.'"

Let it not be supposed that Jacinta stayed in the background in so important a matter as the Catholic priesthood. On the contrary Jacinta was one of those privileged souls who anticipated the recommendation of the Pope in the Encyclical, *"Ad Catholici Sacerdotii"* (On the Catholic Priesthood), of prayers for the sanctification of the clergy. She had a deep understanding of the urgent necessity of prayer for priests.

It was especially toward the end of her life that Jacinta understood better the bond which knitted together her more cherished devotions: the Blessed Sacrament, Our Lady, the work of conversion of sinners, the Holy Father, and prayer for priests in general. Without holy priests it is impossible to work efficiently for the salvation of sinners.

One time she heard that a priest had been forbidden to celebrate Mass. She wept for sorrow, saying that people should not talk about the priests but that rather they should pray for them. For that reason even on her death-bed she asked that prayers be said for that intention. Would that the piety of today were permeated with such a respect and love for the ministers of the altar! May the example of Jacinta bear fruit!

With the express approbation of many of our Most Reverend Prelates, and with the implicit approbation of all of them, the devotion of the Day of the Priesthood is already spreading. In general it is celebrated on the first Saturday or on the first Thursday of the month. To facilitate the practise of this devotion in some dioceses the Day of the Priesthood has been fixed on the first Thursday of the month when it occurs before the First Friday, and on the first Saturday in the other instance. Thus, having been to confession for the First Friday, the people can take part in this other devotion. On those days the faithful assemble in the church for Holy Mass, receive Our Lord in Communion, and take part in other collective exercises of piety, praying for the sanctification of our priests, who spend their lives giving their best for the good of the souls committed to them by Our Lord.

Worldly glory, riches, health, at times even life itself the priest sacrifices for the salvation of souls. Hell and its clients know very well that an exemplary, zealous, and holy clergy is the strongest barrier against the depravity of morals and the undermining of Christian living. Hence the impious war which is waged against it from every side. It is only fair, then, that the faithful should in some way seek to reward the devotion of priests for their souls. Now more than ever before is it necessary to create an intimate bond between the clergy and the faithful. That bond should manifest itself on the part of the faithful in respect for the instruction and guidance given by the priests and in an interest for the salvation and sanctification of the clergy. To this end we must all pray and sacrifice ourselves.

17

Love
for the Pope

The Portuguese have always shown special loyalty to the Holy Father. It was the Pope who emancipated them from vassalage to Castile—and it was to him that the new, little country of Portugal was entrusted at its birth. Though in the course of the centuries this traditional devotion was occasionally weakened, the fault was not the people's. It was the government alone that failed in its duty and fidelity.

Devotion to Christ's Vicar is so deeply rooted in the hearts of the people that no more than a recommendation by two priests was necessary to impress on three little children the importance of this devotion. Jacinta grew to love the Pope intensely. Sister Maria Lúcia de Jesus writes:

"Two priests who came to question us, recommended that we pray for the Holy Father. Jacinta asked who he was; the priests told her and explained his great need of prayers. Jacinta became so devoted to the Holy Father that whenever she offered her sacrifices to Jesus she added the words 'and for the Holy Father.' At the end of the rosary she always said three Hail Marys for the Pope's intentions.

"At times she would say, 'I wish I could see the Holy Father! So many people come here but the Holy Father never does . . .' Naively she supposed that the Holy Father could travel as easily as anyone else.

"Thereafter we offered no prayer or sacrifice to God without praying for the Pope. We conceived such an ardent love for the Holy Father that when the pastor told my mother one day that I might have to go to Rome for questioning by the Pope, I clapped my hands with joy. I said to my cousins, 'Won't it be wonderful to see the Holy Father?'

"But my cousins wept and said, 'We are not able to go—but we can offer this sacrifice for him.' She never again forgot the Pope."

Jacinta kept him always in her prayers and in her sacrifices as is evident from the whole course of her life. Her cousin relates the following:

"Jacinta would tell me at times: 'I feel a very severe pain in my breast but I do not tell mother about it; I want to suffer for the love of Our Lord and in reparation for the sins committed against the Immaculate Heart of Mary, and for the Holy Father and for the conversion of sinners.'"

In health and in illness, at home, in jail, in the hospital, in play and in suffering, Jacinta always remembered the Holy Father. She prayed and made sacrifices for him. She seemed to have a full grasp of the words: *'Ubi Petrus, ibi Ecclesia'* (Where Peter is, i.e., the Pope, there is the Church). Jacinta gave herself without reserve to the Church, represented by the person of the Pope.

Sister Lúcia of Jesus says:

"One day we spent our siesta near the well owned by my parents. Jacinta sat down on the flagstones of the well while Francisco went along with me to find wild honey among the briers of a nearby steep.

"A short while later Jacinta called out, 'Did you see the Holy Father?'

"'No.'

"'I don't know how it happened, but I saw the Holy Father in a very big house, kneeling by a table, with his hands on his face, and he was weeping. Outside the house there were many people. Some of them were throwing stones at him, others were cursing him and saying many ugly words. Poor Holy Father, we must pray very much for him.'

"At another time we went to the cavern on the top of the hill. When we got there, we prostrated on the ground and said the prayers of the Angel.

"Shortly afterward Jacinta got up and said to me, 'Don't you see very many highways and roads and fields full of people weeping and starving for want of food? And the Holy Father in a church praying before the Immaculate Heart of Mary? And many people praying with him?'

"Several days later she asked me, 'Can I tell all those people that I saw the Holy Father?'

"'No. Can't you see that it's part of the secret? You would give it away if you told them that.'

"'Then I won't say anything.'"

One day Lúcia went over to see Jacinta and found her very pensive, sitting on her bed. She asked her what she was thinking about.

"Of the war that is to come. So many people are going to die and most of them are going to hell. Many homes will be destroyed, and many priests will be killed. Look, I am going to heaven. When you see that light at night which the Lady said would come before the war, run up there, too.'

"Don't you know that no one can run to heaven?"

"That's true, you cannot; but don't be afraid. In heaven I shall pray hard for you, for the Holy Father, for Portugal, so that the war may not come here, and for all priests."

In a letter to the Bishop of Leiria concerning the life of Jacinta, Sister Maria Lúcia de Jesus wrote:[11]

"Jacinta was deeply touched by certain things revealed to her in the secret. Because of her great love for the Pope and for sinners she often said, 'Poor Holy Father! I am so sorry for sinners.'"

In interpreting the sentiments of Jacinta, Sister Maria Lúcia pleads fervently:

"May her appeal for prayers for the Holy Father and for priests be heard and put into practice everywhere on earth."

---

11 June 1938.

Obeying the call of the little seer, the pilgrims who flock to Cova da Iria, in Fatima and throughout Portugal, send forth, today more fervently than ever before, a continuous supplication to heaven:

Our Lady of Fatima, bless the Pope!

CHAPTER

18

Attitude of the Family

Our conscience would give us no rest did we let pass the opportunity to refer to the attitude of the parents of the seers toward their children. In cases such as these it is not rare to find the devil, like a bird of prey, attempting to steal the fruits which ought to belong to God alone and to souls. Even the most noble enterprises are at times ruined or rendered useless by his wiles.

The mountain people are generally known to be covetous, but there are exceptions. When the question of acquiring the land for the Shrine arose, some asked as much as 500 *escudos* a square meter for their property.[12] There were others,

---

12 Approximately twenty dollars (at the time, ed.).

however, who facilitated the purchase of their lands, one going so far as to offer a good portion of his property on another location to a man who was clinging fast to his own. Against the parents of the seers the charge of covetousness has never been leveled. Yet, an ounce of prevention is worth a pound of cure and so to avoid any misunderstanding we shall record in this chapter their noble attitude.

When the apparitions began, the Lady recommended the construction of a chapel. At once pilgrims began to contribute for this purpose, placing their alms at the foot of the holm-oak. As the chapel was being built, the contributions came in regularly, though in small quantities. The alms were gathered by a respectable family of the Moita who handed them over to the new Bishop when he later came to the diocese. The family of the seers did not receive a cent. They had enough of their own. The family of Jacinta continued in moderate circumstances, but Lúcia's parents grew poorer. In this regard the Most Reverend José Alves Correia da Silva, Bishop of Leiria, writes:

"We cannot find in them any selfishness or vanity. They accept neither alms nor gifts which the people want to give them. When we decided to direct the works and the religious movement personally, they honestly gave us in the same species the money and other valuable objects which the people in their ardor had left in the place of the apparitions."

Jacinta's parents were well off and today continue to live comfortably; their occupation offered them a living then as it does today. Nothing has changed in their life. On the other hand, the apparitions brought to Lúcia and her family a series of disturbances and losses, for which Lúcia, ironically, had to suffer. This is how she tells it:

"In the bosom of our family there was still another grievance for which I was to blame, as they said. The Cova da Iria was property belonging to my parents. At the rear there was a strip of very fertile land, in which we planted a lot of corn, beans, and vegetables. On the slopes there were a few olive trees, holm-oaks and oak trees. Now, as soon as people began to gather there we could no longer use the land for anything, for the people trampled everything and what little was left was eaten by the pack-animals on which some of the people rode there.

"My mother would complain about this: 'Now when you want to eat, go ask that Lady for food'; to which my sisters would add, 'Now you ought to eat only what is cultivated in the Cova da Iria.' These words wounded me so much that it was extremely difficult for me to take up a piece of bread to eat.

"To the tormenting thoughts of the total loss of the Cova da Iria, which was good pasture land for our flocks, and of the edibles which were harvested there, was added the useless questioning due to the conviction that the happenings were nothing else than the simple chimeras and fantasies of childish imaginations. One of my sisters did almost nothing else than take my place with the flock while I came home to be interviewed by those who sought me. This loss of time would mean nothing to a wealthy family, but for us who had to live from our work it was something considerable. Very shortly my mother was forced to sell the flock, a move which was harmful to the family support. In moments of crisis all this was thrown in my face. I hope Our Lord accepted everything, since I always offered it to Him, happy to sacrifice for Him and sinners.

"One of the neighbors one day said that some gentleman had given me a certain sum of money. My mother immediately called me and asked for it. I answered that I had received no money from anyone, but she insisted that I hand it to her and to persuade me she used the broomstick. After she had shaken the dust off my clothing to the last speck, one of my sisters intervened; Carolina, for it was she, and a neighbor named Virginia, who also intervened, confessed that they had been present at the interview with those gentlemen and that they had seen that nothing was given to me. After that defense I was able to retire to my beloved well and there to offer to God this sacrifice."

The attitude of the parents of the children cannot but leave a profound impression. They did not create Fatima; they were not to enjoy it. After the Lady appeared, Senhora Maria Rosa, Lúcia's mother, lived for twenty-five years the same obscure life that had been hers before the apparitions, devoted to the cares of the home and of her children and then, after a prolonged suffering, she died in the Lord. It should be noted that even though she had been ill for months in the house of her children, she asked to be taken to her home and died in Lúcia's very room on the day of the Feast of Our Lady of Mount Carmel.

And Jacinta's parents, showing the signs of the years that have passed, live humbly and modestly, as they did twenty-five years ago, unknown in the midst of the multitudes which tenderly and with tears sing the glories and the blessings of Mary showered upon us by means of their children.

Their only ambition is that which Sister Maria Lúcia expresses as she closes the narrative of so many wonders:

"Here we are, Most Reverend Bishop, on the 13th of October. Your Excellency knows all that transpired on that day. The words of this apparition which were most deeply engraved in my heart were those of the request of Our Most Holy heavenly Mother:

"*Do not offend God, our Lord, any more because He is already grievously offended!*'

"What a loving complaint and what a tender request! Would that it echoed throughout the world and that all the children of the Mother of Heaven should hear the sound of her voice!"

The Mystery of Light

How grateful we must be to God for the edifying example which His Divine Mercy presents in the life and virtues of Jacinta! As we examine and observe it, we notice more and more the profound influence of grace, the mysterious transformations which are wrought in her soul by the light of the Holy Spirit. The life of Jacinta grows in perfection, rising ever higher and higher, just as so often during her life as shepherdess her gaze had traveled aloft and roved over the cliffs in searching scrutiny of the horizon.

Through the inspired eyes of the soul she looks out upon new vistas incomparably more beautiful than all that her mortal eyes had ever contemplated on this earth and all that her little heart had heretofore loved so intensely. Her soul, though torn and bleeding, rises and frees itself even of her love for parents and brothers, and such is her eagerness to fly to heaven that earth and family are almost forgotten.

"Shortly before she died I asked her," states Senhora Maria da Purificação Godinho, "if she wished to see her mother again. She answered that her family would not live much longer, and that soon they would all meet in heaven."

If we think of the Jacinta who wept in jail because she was far away from her parents, if we contemplate the same Jacinta who was filled with sadness and longing because she was going to die alone in a hospital, and if we later see her detached from the world, from life and from her very family, we can appreciate more readily the radical transformation which took place in this soul as she was engulfed and submerged in the light from above. On October 13, 1917, the day of the great final apparition, as the throngs pressed together in order the more easily to see and hear what was going on, the bystanders had to protect the children lest they be crushed. Jacinta, distracted and filled with fear, cried because of the pushing and shoving she was enduring. Lúcia caressed her and asked her not to cry, assuring her that no one would harm her. It is this same Jacinta who after the apparitions recommended to her cousin:

"Do not tell the secret, not even if they kill you!"

Like the Apostles coming out of the Upper Room, Jacinta was filled with the strength which the Holy Spirit confers. It was through an extraordinary supernatural gift that there was bestowed on this little child, who later became so sickly, the type of Christian courage and fortitude which characterized the martyrs and all of God's chosen ones, and which puts to shame so many Christians of today who are dominated by a false shame and by human respect. Lúcia gives us in happy contrast the note of simple courage in the seers as opposed to the misgivings of their families. About the same day, the 13th of October, she writes:

"The rumor had spread that the authorities were to explode a bomb close to us at the time of the apparition. I was not in the least afraid, and when I saw my cousins, I told them, exclaiming, 'How wonderful to be given the grace to ascend to heaven from there with Our Lady!"

"My parents, however, were very much afraid, and for the first time they wished to accompany me, saying, 'If our daughter is going to die, we want to die with her.'

"My father then took me by the hand to the very place of the apparition, but I did not see him again until I returned home that night."

In jail Jacinta had wept because she was to die without seeing her parents. Then it had been the old Jacinta—nature without grace.

"The prisoners who witnessed this scene wanted to console us. 'Why,' they said, 'do you not tell the secret to the Administrator? What difference does it make if the Lady does not want you to tell it?'

"'Never,' answered Jacinta resolutely, 'I would rather die.'

"This is Jacinta transformed. Now there is light—nature under the impulse of grace.

When Lúcia was to be taken to the Administration for an interview, and so notified her cousins, Jacinta told her calmly, "I am going to get up immediately and call Francisco. We are going to your well to pray fervently for you—when you come back, meet us there."

"When I returned I stopped at the well, and there they were, the two of them, praying. As soon as they saw me, Jacinta hastened to embrace me, and asked me how I had made out.

"I told them, and she said, 'Do you see? We must not fear anything. The Lady always helps us. She is such a friend to us! . . .'"

The clearest proof of the inner transformation of Jacinta, however, is found in her life of mortification and sacrifice as revealed in the following pages which speak of her illness and death.

Heavenward

The same illness that had overtaken Francisco now sent Jacinta to bed. The whole family was ill. Influenza was already taking its terrible toll. They placed Jacinta first in the room where she had been born, then they moved her to the room at the left as one enters the house through the front door. Lúcia writes:

"She recovered somewhat. She was able to get up, but spent the days sitting on her little brother's bed. One day she sent for me in a hurry. I ran over to her bedside, and she said to me:

"'Our Lady came to see us and said that she is coming very soon for Francisco to take him up to heaven. But she asked me if I still wanted to convert more sinners. I told her that I did. She told me that I was going to a hospital, and that I was going to suffer very much there, and that I should suffer for the conversion of sinners, in reparation for the sins committed against the Immaculate Heart of Mary and for the love of Jesus.'

"Being of stronger constitution, or perhaps because God was calling her to greater sufferings, Jacinta managed to get up, but she never recovered completely. A growth appeared on her left side, which in time burst, allowing pus to flow freely. She would bend over a little piece of broken crockery into which the pus could fall. Often she would go to sleep in this position. A purulent pleurisy was the cause of her suffering.

"She was sent to the Hospital of Saint Augustine in Vila Nova de Ourém, where she remained for two whole months, July and August of 1919. There was no improvement. She returned home, where death approached gradually.

"She knew that her going to the hospitals of Vila Nova de Ourém and of Lisbon would not bring recovery but rather more suffering. Long before anyone spoke to her about entering the hospital of Vila Nova de Ourém she told me:

"'Our Lady wants me to go to two hospitals, but it is not to be cured; it is only to suffer more for the love of Our Lord and for sinners.'

"I do not know the exact words Our Lady spoke to her in these apparitions, for I never inquired about them. I contented myself with listening to her own account of them.

"She returned to her parents' home with a large open sore on her side. Dressing it daily caused her much pain, but she uttered no complaint, and never gave the slightest sign of disgust. Her greatest suffering came from the frequent visits and questionings by the persons who came to see her, from whom she could no longer hide herself.

"'I offer this sacrifice for sinners,' she would say with resignation. 'I wish I could go to the top of the hill and say the rosary again in our little place! But I cannot do it any more. When you go to the Cova da Iria, pray for me. I will never go there again.'"

As the body wasted away, the soul's vision became clearer and purer in the light of approaching eternity. Her cousin reveals beautiful things of the little victim who immolated herself, and of the consummation of the sacrifice. She writes:

"Shortly before she fell ill, Jacinta said, 'I have a terrible headache, and I am very thirsty, but I do not want to drink. I want to suffer for sinners.'

"All the time I had free from school or from my other duties I spent with my two companions.

"One day as I stopped by on my way to school, Jacinta said to me, 'Listen! Tell the Hidden Jesus that I like Him, that I love Him very much.'

"At other times she would say, 'Tell Jesus that I send Him my love, and that I long to see Him.'

"Whenever I visited her room first, she used to say, 'Now go and see Francisco; I will make the sacrifice of staying here alone.'

"She loved to have Francisco at her side. . . ."

At times Lúcia stayed away for a long time doing errands. "Upon returning I would run to her, and hear her say, 'Please do not go again. I missed you very much. Ever since you left I did not speak to anyone. I do not know how to talk to other people.'

"I loved to go to the Cabeço as often as I could to pray in our favorite cavern. Jacinta loved flowers, and so, on my way back, I used to pick a bouquet of lilies and peonies, if it were the proper season, and bring them to her.

"'They are from the Cabeço,' I would say.

"Sometimes she cried as she took them, and said, 'I am never going back there, neither to Valinhos nor to the Cova da Iria, and I miss them so much!'

"'But what does that matter to you, now that you are going to heaven to see Our Lord and Our Lady?'

"'That's right,' she would answer, and then happily plucked off the petals one by one to count them.

"A few days after she fell ill, she gave me the rope she used and said to me, 'Keep it for me; I am afraid my mother may see it. If I get better I want it back again!'

"This rope had three knots and was somewhat bloodstained. I kept it hidden away until finally I left my mother's house; afterward, not knowing what to do with it, I burned it with that of her little brother.

"When her mother would look sad at seeing her so ill, she would say, 'Don't worry, mother, I am going to heaven. There I shall pray hard for you.'

"At other times she would say, 'Don't cry, mother, I am well.'

"When someone would ask her whether she needed anything, she would say, 'I am very thirsty but I do not want to drink. I offer it up to Jesus for sinners.'

"One day when my aunt was asking me many questions, Jacinta called me and said, 'I don't want you to tell anyone that I am suffering, not even my mother: I do not want her to worry.'

"Another day I found her hugging a picture of Our Lady and saying, 'O my dear Mother in heaven, do I have to die alone?'

"The poor child seemed frightened at the thought of dying alone. I tried to comfort her.

"'What difference does it make if you die alone, so long as Our Lady is coming for you?'

"'That's right. I will not mind. But somehow I don't always remember that she is coming for me.'

"On another occasion her mother brought her a glass of milk and asked her to take it.

"'I don't want it, mother,' she answered, and pushed the glass away with her little hand.

"My aunt insisted for a while, and then left the room not knowing what to do, for, as she said, 'Jacinta has no appetite.'

"As soon as we were alone, I asked her, 'Jacinta, how is it that you disobey your mother like this? Why don't you offer this sacrifice to Our Lord?'

"At this she shed a few tears which I had the happiness of drying, and then said, 'I did not remember to.'

"She called her mother then, asked her forgiveness, and told her that she was ready to take whatever she wanted her to. Her mother brought back the glass of milk, and Jacinta drank it down without showing the slightest repugnance. Then she told me, 'If you only knew how hard it was to drink that!'

"Some time later she told me, 'It is becoming harder and harder for me to drink milk and broth, but I do not say anything. I take them all for the love of Our Lord and of the Immaculate Heart of Mary, our dear Heavenly Mother.'

"Knowing how disagreeable milk was to Jacinta, her mother one day brought with the milk a bunch of delicious grapes.

"'Look, Jacinta,' she said, 'If you cannot drink the milk let it go and eat the grapes.'

"'No, mother, I don't want the grapes. Please take them away. I would rather have the milk.'

"And without showing the slightest sign of repugnance she drank it. My aunt left satisfied, supposing that the child's appetite was returning.

"Jacinta then looked at me and said, 'I was dying to eat those grapes, and it was very hard for me to drink that milk. But I wanted to offer that sacrifice to Our Lord.'

"One morning I found her very pale, and asked her if she felt worse.

"'I had much pain last night, and I wanted to offer Our Lord the sacrifice of not turning in bed, so I did not sleep at all.'

"Another time she told me, 'When I am alone I get down from the bed to say the prayers of the Angel, but now I cannot touch the floor with my head because I fall down, and so I kneel and pray.'

"Again, I asked her one time, 'Are you better?'

"'You know very well that I shall not get better,' she replied, and added, 'My chest pains so much, but I don't say anything. I am suffering for the conversion of sinners.'

"One day when I went to see her she asked me, 'Have you made any sacrifices today? I have made many. My mother went away and I wanted to see Francisco many times, but I did not go.'

"My aunt made this request of me once: 'Ask Jacinta what she thinks when she covers her face with her hands and remains motionless for so long. I have already asked her, but she smiles and does not answer.'

"I put the question to Jacinta.

"'I think of Our Lord, of Our Lady, and of this . . . [she mentioned parts of the secret]. I love to think about them!

"I gave this answer to my aunt, who remarked to my mother, 'I cannot understand this. The life of these children is a puzzle.'

"And my mother added, 'So it is. When they are by themselves they talk in such low tones that we cannot get a single word no matter how closely we listen, and as soon as someone approaches they turn their heads and say no more. I cannot understand this mysteriousness either.'

"Once again the Blessed Virgin deigned to visit Jacinta, to announce to her new crosses and new sacrifices. Jacinta gave me the news, saying:

"'She told me I am going to Lisbon to another hospital; that I will not see you again nor my parents; that after much suffering I will die alone, but that I must not be afraid since she herself is coming to take me to heaven.'

"She hugged me and wept. 'I will never see you again. You are not going to visit me there. Pray, pray hard for me. I am going to die alone.'

"When at last the day of her departure for Lisbon arrived, her suffering was intense.

"Repeatedly she hugged me, and in the midst of her tears cried, 'I will never see you again, nor my mother, nor my brothers, nor my father. I will never see anybody again. And then I am going to die alone. . . .'

"'Don't think about it,' I advised.

"'But I should think about it, because the more I think the more I suffer, and I want to suffer for the love of Our Lord and for sinners; anyway, I don't mind. Our Lady is going there to take me to heaven.'

"At times she would pray: 'O Jesus, now you can convert many sinners because this sacrifice is very big.'

"From time to time she would ask me, 'Am I really going to die without receiving the Hidden Jesus? I wish Our Lady would bring Him to me when she comes for me.'

"One day, when I asked her, 'What are you going to do in heaven?' she replied, 'I am going to love Jesus very much, also the Immaculate Heart of Mary; I am going to pray for you, for sinners, for the Holy Father, for my parents and brothers, and for all those who have asked me to pray for them.'

"She would speak very enthusiastically of Our Lord and of Our Lady: 'I love to suffer for their sakes. They love very much those who suffer for the conversion of sinners.'"

The last days of Jacinta's life were spent in intimate union with the Mother of God. Because the Lady told her before she entered the hospital that she was going to die, Jacinta objected to surgical treatment. A successful operation was performed, however—and yet Jacinta grew worse. Violent pains racked her little body. Then as if by magic, four days before she died, the pains disappeared. Jacinta explained that Our Lady had again visited her, promising that in a short time she would come for her and relieve her of all pain. From that day until the moment of her death she showed no more signs of suffering.

The Lady told her that the sin which leads most people to perdition is the sin of impurity; that luxuries have to be put aside, and that people must not be obstinate in sin as they have been until now; that people must perform great penances. The Lady was very sad as she said these words.

"For that reason Jacinta used to say again and again, 'Oh, I feel so sorry for Our Lady! I feel so sorry for her!'"

Becoming worse and worse, and knowing that she was about to die, Jacinta asked for the last Sacraments, but received only the Sacrament of Penance. Hers was not the consolation of receiving Our Lord before death. On the very day of her confession she died peacefully.

They dressed her in white as for First Holy Communion, with a blue bow, in accordance with her wishes, as she wanted to be buried in the garb of Our Lady. The coffin was placed in the sacristy of the Church of the Angels. Many people desired to touch her with religious articles, but in order to avoid this, the pastor locked the coffin in the office. Afterward, for greater safety, he left it in the care of the Confraternity of the Blessed Sacrament and deposited the key with the undertaker. Yet the pilgrims continued to come with great respect and in perfect order.

On the 24th of February, three days after her death, the body was placed in a lead coffin, which was properly sealed. It was then accompanied to the station, and from there it passed through Chāo de Maçās, to the cemetery of Vila Nova de Ourém, where it rested until its removal to the cemetery of Fatima.

21

With God

Very soon people began to pray to Jacinta. It was thought, and with good reason, that her request would be more readily heeded, for God always hears more promptly the prayer of the innocent. And if to innocence penance is joined, as well as reparation and immolation for the sins of others, then there is nothing that God can refuse. I sincerely believe that here on earth, and now in heaven, the prayer of little Jacinta is most powerful with God and with Our Lady. Nor is evidence of this power lacking, for the Baron of Alvaiázere speaks clearly of many favors obtained for his family through the intercession of her whose mortal remains he so tenderly sheltered for years in his family sepulcher. Maria da Purificação Godinho also writes that already several extraordinary favors have been obtained through the intercession of Jacinta.

Lúcia herself tells us the following:

"There was a woman in our neighborhood who always insulted us whenever we met her. We came upon her one day as she was coming out of a tavern, and, since the poor thing was somewhat intoxicated, she was not satisfied with mere insults.

"After she finished her work, Jacinta told me, 'We have to ask Our Lady and offer sacrifices for the conversion of this woman. She says so many sinful things that unless she goes to confession she will go to hell.'

"A few days later we ran by the door of this woman.

"Suddenly Jacinta stopped in her tracks, and, turning back, she asked, 'Listen! Is it tomorrow that we are going to see the Lady?'

"'Yes, it is.'

"'Then let us not play any more. Let us make this sacrifice for the conversion of sinners.'

"And without realizing that someone might be watching her, she raised prayerfully her little hands and eyes to heaven and made the offering. The woman meanwhile was peeking through a shutter in the house, and witnessed this action. Later she told my mother that the conduct of Jacinta had so impressed her that she needed no other proof to believe in the reality of the apparitions and that henceforth she not only would not insult us, but would continually ask us to pray to Our Lady to obtain forgiveness for her sins.

"Again, a poor woman afflicted with a terrible disease met us one day, and weeping, she knelt before Jacinta and begged her to ask Our Lady to cure her. When Jacinta saw the woman kneeling before her, she was troubled, and with trembling hands she tried to lift her. Seeing that she could not do it, she, too, knelt down, and said three Hail Marys with the woman. Then she asked her to arise, and said that Our Lady would cure her. She continued to pray daily for that woman, until some time later she returned to thank Our Lady for her cure.

"Another time it was a soldier who wept like a child. He had received orders to rejoin his regiment, and had to leave his wife who was sick and three children. He asked for the cure of his wife, or the recall of the order. Jacinta invited him to recite the rosary with her. Then she told him, 'Do not weep. Our Lady is very good—certainly she will grant you the grace you ask for.'

"From that time on, at the end of the rosary she always said a Hail Mary for him. Several months later he appeared with his wife and his three children to thank Our Lady for the two favors he had received. Because of a fever he had contracted the day before he was to leave, he had been freed from military service, and his wife, he said, had been cured by a miracle of Our Lady.

"The first time that Senhora Emilia da Soutaria came to take me to the house of the Vicar at Olival, Jacinta went with me. When we arrived at the village where the good widow lived, it was night, but in spite of that the news of our arrival spread rapidly, and the house of Senhora Emilia was immediately surrounded by many people. They wanted to see us, to ask us questions and favors.

"One of them, a pious woman who was wont to say the rosary in her house with other devout villagers, came to invite us to her house to say the rosary with them. We tried to excuse ourselves, saying that we would say it with Senhora Emilia, but she was so insistent that we could not help but yield to her request. When this news got out, the people flocked to the house of the good woman in order to secure a place there, and so the way was left free for us.

"As we were on the way, a girl of about twenty years of age came out to meet us. Weeping, she knelt down and asked us to come into her house to say a Hail Mary for the cure of her father, who for more than three years had not been able to find any rest from an attack of continuous hiccoughs. It was impossible to resist a plea of this kind. I helped the poor girl to get up, and, since the night was already well spent (we were carrying two lanterns to find our way), I told Jacinta to stay there while I would go to say the rosary with the other people, and that on my return I would stop for her. She consented, and went into the house.

"On my way back, I, too, entered the house, and there found Jacinta sitting in a chair in front of a man who was also seated. Not very old, but emaciated and weeping with emotion, he was surrounded by a few other persons, who, I thought, were the family. As Jacinta saw me, she arose, said good-bye, and promised that she would not forget him in her prayers. Then we returned to the house of Senhora Emilia.

"On the following day we left early in the morning for Olival, but returned three days later.

As we arrived at the house of Senhora Emilia, we met the happy girl accompanied by her father, who now looked much better, his nervousness and extreme weakness having disappeared. They came to give thanks for the grace received, for, they said, the annoying hiccoughs had not returned. Afterward, whenever I passed by their home, that good family always expressed their gratitude and said that our friend was completely cured.

"My aunt Vitória, who lived in Fatima, had a son who was truly a prodigal. I do not know why, but he had left his father's house, and no one knew what had happened to him. In her affliction, my aunt came to Aljustrel one day to ask me to pray to Our Lady for her son. Not finding me, she made the request to Jacinta, who promised to pray for him. A few days later, the boy showed up at home, and asked pardon of his parents, and then went to Aljustrel to tell his unfortunate story.

"He said that after having spent all that he had stolen, he had roamed about for some time until he was put in jail at Torres Novas. After having been there for a while, he succeeded in escaping one night and fled to the mountains, to the trackless pine forests. Thinking himself completely lost,

and torn between the fear of being captured and
the darkness of a stormy night, he found only one
recourse, and that was prayer. Falling on his knees,
he began to pray. A few minutes later Jacinta
appeared to him, took him by the hand, and led
him to the road which goes from Alqueidão to
Reguengo, indicating to him that he should follow that road. When morning came, he found
himself on the way to Boleiros. He recognized the
spot where he was, and, deeply moved, directed
his steps to his father's house.

"He affirmed unswervingly that Jacinta had
appeared to him, and that he had recognized her
perfectly. I asked Jacinta if she had really gone to
him. She answered that she had not, that she did
not even know the location of those pine forests
and mountains where he had been.

"'I only prayed and begged Our Lady very
much for him because I was sorry for aunt Vitória.'

"That was what she said to me.—How, then,
did it happen? I do not know—God knows."

As he left Fatima on May 13, 1938, His
Eminence the Cardinal Patriarch of Lisbon did
not wish to depart without visiting the tomb of
Jacinta. There he implored her protection, his soul
filled with the imperishable impressions of those

days, and deeply stirred by the reading of the life of Jacinta.

The venerable hierarchy visited at night the tomb of Jacinta for the closing exercises of their last spiritual retreat, many of the bishops making the journey on foot.

At the end of the retreat for the Catholic Action leaders of the diocese of Leiria, which takes place every year at Fatima, the young men asked in one of the last gatherings to visit the tomb of the seer. Seventy boys around the white tomb, their faces illumined in the glow of the lanterns, listening in silence to an invocation to that lovely child, whom Our Lady sent us so providentially to be the light of Catholic Action, was a sight not easily forgotten. They begged on their knees for the triumph of Catholic Action, through the merits of the heroic little girl whose mortal remains lay before them. For Jacinta is like a token, a pledge offered to Catholic Action by her who was chosen as its Godmother and Protectress.

From everywhere we are receiving inspiring news of the beneficent influence exercised on the souls of children and of adults by the reading of the life of this chosen soul. Her tomb is a place of pilgrimage for both the great and the lowly. Her name is reverently pronounced in intercession, and already the efficacy of these prayers has been manifested in abundant favors and graces.

The Fragrance of Christ

Heretofore Lúcia, who has survived her two little cousins, has been merely a chronicler. But we wanted to ascertain her impression of Jacinta's personality. Was her virtue like that of the flower whose fragrance lies hidden in delicacy, or was it apparent to all who knew her? This is Lúcia's answer to our question:

"How did people feel in Jacinta's presence? Much, I think, as anyone feels in the presence of a saintly person who seems always to be in union with God. In everything Jacinta did she seemed to practice the presence of God to the degree of older persons far advanced in virtue.

"She was always friendly, though serious and reserved toward all. I never noticed in her any great love for games or toys such as one generally finds in children. [This in regard to Jacinta after the apparition.] I cannot say that the other children gathered around her as they did around me; this was most probably due, however, to the fact that she did not know as many songs or stories with which to amuse them. Then too, there was in her a quality of seriousness far beyond her age. If in her presence a child or even a grown-up were to say or to do anything unseemly, she would reprimand him and say, 'Do not do that, you offend the Lord our God, and He is already very much offended.' And when, as sometimes happened, the guilty party retorted angrily that she was only a hypocrite,[13] Jacinta would simply stare sternly at the speaker and walk away in silence. For this reason, perhaps, she did not enjoy more popularity.

"When the children were with Jacinta, however, they seemed to enjoy her company. They would hug and kiss her with all of their innocent tenderness; they loved to sing and play with her, calling out—if she were not present—for me to bring her to them. If I would tell them that she did not want to come since they were bad children, they would promise to

---

13 Beata falsa ou Santinha de pau carunchento.

be good if only she came along. 'Go get her,' they pleaded, 'tell her that we shall be good if she comes.'

"During her illness I found that there was always a large group waiting at her door, hoping to gain admittance with me, but of themselves they held back through a sort of awe. As I left I would ask Jacinta if she wished to have some of them stay with her as company.

"'All right,' she agreed, 'but only those who are smaller than I.'

"She would entertain her company by teaching them the Our Father, the Hail Mary, and the Sign of the Cross. Generally she would say the rosary with them and beg them not to offend Our Lord lest they should go to hell. Often too, they would sing or play marbles with the apples, chestnuts, and sweet acorns that my aunt always supplied in great abundance. In this fashion some of the children would spend almost the whole day with Jacinta; yet once they left her presence they seemed afraid to return without an invitation. They would wait for me to ask them in, or perhaps wait by the door of the house until my aunt or Jacinta herself should invite them in.

"Without exception the grown-up persons who visited Jacinta admired her calm, resigned patience. Generally she would remain just in the position her mother left her. Although she often remained silent and sad toward the visitors, yet she never showed the least impatience with the detailed and fatiguing interviews.

"Her only comment was made to me after the interviews were finished, 'My head was aching so much from listening to those people! Since I cannot run and hide, I offer these sacrifices to our Lord!'

"Among her visitors were neighbors who came to sew at her bedside. 'I'm going to work near Jacinta,' they would say, 'I don't know why it is but I like to be near her.' Sometimes they took their children too so that they might play with Jacinta while they plied their sewing more busily.

"To the questions and remarks of these neighbors the little girl would respond briefly, yet always in words full of love, begging them, 'Don't let your children commit sins, they may go to hell because of you.'

"Or in reference to adults she would say, 'Tell them not to do that, it is a sin. They offend God, they may be lost.'

"People from afar off, even those who came more from curiosity than devotion, seemed to sense the same supernatural air about Jacinta. At times they would remark to me, 'We have just come from talking with Jacinta and Francisco. One feels something of the supernatural in their presence.'

"One priest said, 'I was impressed by the innocence and sincerity of Jacinta and her little brother. Unless she contradicts herself, I shall believe her!'

"And his companion added, 'I do not know how to describe my feelings in the presence of those two children. It seems that something of the supernatural is with them. It did my heart good to speak to them.'"

Such is the testimony of Sister Lúcia, Jacinta's first cousin and moreover the first and principal recipient of the vision.

How admirable is God in His saints! In the soul of Jacinta there fell one day the seed of divine grace. So well did it germinate, grow, and fructify that today throughout the world men give glory to God in heaven for the fragrance of Christ that blossomed forth in the soul of this generous child.

CHAPTER

23

The Punishment
of God?

The trials and misfortunes which from time to time visit nations have a punitive function which Divine Justice applies to man's violation of God's laws. Individuals receive punishment in this world or in the next, because the soul is immortal. With nations, the same is not true. Their existence, like their end or purpose, is merely temporal. They have no immortal soul. Only in this life can punishment be meted out to the collectivity. Hence, the successive transfer of empires which is constantly found in the words of the prophets and in the history of the Hebrew people. After all, in what does the history of Israel consist? It is an impressive alternation—now a great internal prosperity, with a splendid external success, now the most wretched life, with the loss of independence itself. It all hinged on the way in which the law of God was obeyed. Tottering thrones, dispersed and scattered nations, lost empires, dark hours of defeat and oppression, shameful pages of history: all are in the hands of God—punishments due to the neglect of His precepts, His laws, His dispositions. Today, as yesterday, as always!

Our Lady appeared in Fatima twenty-eight years ago, and asked for an amendment of life, a change of morals, and reparation for sins committed. What has been our answer to her? Can we say that everything has been done? Not long ago, the grave and solemn voice of the teaching Church, in a collective pastoral of our venerable Portuguese hierarchy, on the occasion of the silver jubilee of the apparitions, openly admitted that we have not done so. What are we waiting for? The mercy of God may grow tired, and the hour of justice arrive. For the rest of the world it has arrived. Can it not come for us also? We cannot trifle with God.

When, in May of 1938, we sent to Sister Maria Lúcia of Jesus a copy of the first edition of *Jacinta,* so that she might make her comments, she answered the following month in a long letter to the Bishop of Leiria concerning the great secret:

"In fact, Most Reverend Bishop, Jacinta was deeply touched with a few things revealed to us in the secret, and because of her great love of the Holy Father and of sinners, she said many times, 'Poor Holy Father! I am so sorry for sinners!'

"And I add now that were she living at this time, when these things are so close at hand, how much more would she be impressed! If the world only knew the moment of grace which is still granted to it to repent! Would that her recommendation of prayers for the Holy Father and for priests were heeded and practised in every corner of the earth! Your Excellency, you are doubtlessly surprised to read these few words from me, which seem to indicate something pending, but it is not I who speak them. It is Our Lord Who is using me. Your Excellency may use them as Our Lady may inspire you."

Why was this not published in the second edition which was printed immediately afterward? It did not seem opportune at the time. The allusion to the war which was to break out shortly is clear. Today there is all around us added evidence of the necessity of penance, as demanded by God and asked so repeatedly by the Heavenly Mother. But before going any further, let us cite a recent letter of Lúcia to the Bishop of Leiria in which she revealed two parts of the secret:

"Your Excellency is aware that a few years ago God manifested that sign which the astronomers designated by the name of the Aurora Borealis. God used that phenomenon to make me understand that His justice was ready to deal the blow upon the guilty nations, and for that reason I began to insist on the atoning Communion on the First Saturday of every month, and on the consecration of Russia to the Immaculate Heart of Mary. My purpose was to obtain mercy and pardon and forgiveness for the whole world, but especially for Europe. God, in His infinite mercy, gradually let me feel that the terrible moment was approaching. And Your Excellency is aware that on opportune occasions I indicated it. I still say that the prayers offered and penances done in Portugal have not placated the Divine Justice, because they have not been accompanied by contrition and amendment. I hope that Jacinta intercedes for us in heaven.

"At times Jacinta would say, 'What a pity! If people stopped offending God, the war would not come, and they would not go to hell. I am sorry for you. Francisco and I are going to heaven, but you are going to stay here alone. I asked Our Lady to take you also to heaven, but she wants you to stay here for some time. When the war comes, don't be afraid. In heaven I will pray for you.'

"Shortly before she left for Lisbon, in one of her moments of loneliness, I told her, 'Don't be sorry that I am not going with you. It won't be long. You can spend that time thinking about Our Lady, about Our Lord, and in saying those words you like so well, "My God, I love you; Immaculate Heart of Mary, Sweet Heart of Mary."'

"'That's good,' she answered with spirit, 'I will never get tired of saying that until I die, and after that I will sing it in heaven for ever.'

"Your Excellency, someone may think that I should have revealed these things long ago, because in their opinion they would have had double value then. So it would have been if God had wanted to give me to the world as a prophetess, but I believe that such was not God's purpose in manifesting these things to me. If this were the case, I think that when in 1917 He told me to be silent, an order which was confirmed by those who represented Him, He would rather have ordered me to speak. I think, therefore, Most Reverend Bishop, that God wanted only to use me to *remind* the world of the necessity of avoiding sin, and of making reparation to the offended God through prayer and penance."

What has God in store for us? Portugal has been, until today, and for many years, the object of the particular mercy of God. The conditions for its continuance are clear. We merely want to add here, as a documentary note, the tremendous punishment which was going to fall, and which will fall upon our land if the required reparation is not made. The following is an excerpt from a letter of the Reverend Doctor Manuel Nunes Formigão, Jr., to the Bishop of Leiria, in which he explains the nature of the punishment threatened in the secret of Jacinta:

"Revelation which, according to Jacinta de Jesus Marto, the Most Blessed Virgin made to her when she was in Lisbon, shortly before her death, and which because she could not do it personally, as she so eagerly desired, her godmother, Dona Maria da Purificação Godinho, a lady whom I have ascertained to be most trustworthy, transmitted to me from her by order of Our Lady:

"Our Lord is deeply angry with the sins and crimes which are committed in Portugal. For that reason a terrible cataclysm of the social order threatens our land, and especially the city of Lisbon. There will break out, it seems, a civil war of an anarchist or Communistic character, followed by sacks, slaughters, and devastations of every kind. The capital will be converted into a true image of hell. At the time when offended Divine Justice shall inflict such a frightful punishment, all those who are able, let them flee from that city. This punishment now predicted, it is fitting that it should be pronounced, little by little and with due discretion.

"What has been written here is a free rendition, but as exact as possible, of the communication of the seer."

May this not be an allusion to the Communistic invasion by which we were threatened, and which our venerable Bishops and Prelates asked the Blessed Virgin to avert from us, and for which they later came to thank her in a national pilgrimage? One question: Is the required reparation already made?

Is the intensification of the religious life which is noted in Portugal the reparation? Also, the characteristic note of penance of the pilgrimages to Fatima, a magnificent example of which was the journey of 10,000 boys, many of whom came from afar on foot, as well as the triumphant reception of the image of Our Lady in its journey to Lisbon—are these the reparation?

There is still very much to do. May a legion of souls, innocent and burning with love for God and for neighbor, rise up in imitation of that noble figure of Jacinta, and take upon itself the charge, like victims of a holocaust, of meriting, through a life of prayer and suffering, forgiveness for the sins and iniquities of our country. Suffering for the sake of suffering is foolishness, but to suffer for the love of God and for souls is the sublime contagion of that peerless folly which led God to become man, and to suffer the most cruel and the most shameful martyrdom for the love of us.

The Peace
of the Cloister

Lúcia remained alone while Jacinta climbed through Calvary to the bliss of Tabor. Lúcia speaks thus of her own sentiments:

"What sadness I felt when I found myself alone! In a very short time Our Lord took to heaven my beloved father, then Francisco, and now Jacinta, whom I shall never see again in this world.

"As soon as I was able, I retired to the Cabeço and hid in the cavern of the cliff, so that there, alone with God, I might give vent to my sorrow and shed abundantly the tears of my grief. And as I came down the slope, everything reminded me of my beloved companions: the stones on which we sat so many times, the flowers which I no longer picked because I had no one to give them to, and the Valinhos, where we had enjoyed together the delights of paradise.

"As though doubting the reality and half-distracted, I entered one day into the house of my aunt, and went directly to the room of Jacinta, calling for her. Her sister Teresa, seeing me like this, stopped me on the way, saying that Jacinta was no longer there. Shortly after, the news arrived that she had taken flight to heaven, and then they brought her body to Vila Nova de Ourém. My aunt took me to see the mortal remains of her little daughter, in the hope of distracting me in that manner, but for a long time my sadness seemed to increase more and more."

There was nothing else to do in the land where her eyes had opened to the light of day, and where they had the pleasure of foretasting the delights of heaven in a sweet vision of the Mother of God. Lúcia too had to die. She resolved, with her parents' consent, to retire to the silence of the cloister, to the peace of the convent. Everything was prepared, and the day was set for the journey. Lúcia, who was still keeping her secret, said good-bye to those beloved things which had been silent witnesses of so many marvels; it was a tender parting. This is how she describes it:

"In the pale light of the moon, already risen, I said good-bye to my well, and to the old yard, where so many times I had spent long hours contemplating the beautiful starry sky and the marvels of the rising and the setting of the sun. The sun at times charmed me by making its rays gleam on the drops of dew which in the morning covered the mountains like pearls, and in the afternoons it often played upon the puffs of snow hanging from the pine trees, reminding one of the beauties of paradise.

"Without saying good-bye to anybody, on the following day, accompanied by my mother and a poor working-man from Leiria named Manuel Correia, I departed, carrying the secret inviolate. We passed by the Cova da Iria, so that I might say my final farewell. For the last time I said my rosary there, and as long as I could see the place, I kept turning back, as if to say one more good-bye.

"We arrived at Leiria about nine in the morning, and there I met Senhora D. Philomena Miranda, later my Confirmation sponsor, who was charged with accompanying me. The train was to leave at two o'clock in the afternoon, and at the station I gave my poor mother my farewell embrace. There I left her bathed in a flood of tears at the parting. The train started, and with it went my poor heart, submerged in a sea of *saudades* and memories, which I found impossible to forget."

* * *

The child model which Our Lord has given us, of whose life we have drawn but a pale sketch (for only in heaven shall we know it fully), cannot be forgotten. May the name and example of Jacinta reach every corner of Portugal and the world, and may she be presented for imitation to the children of our schools, colleges, eucharistic crusades, cathechetical groups, and beginners in Catholic Action (*Benjaminas*)!

Making Fatima the altar of propitiation for all Portugal, working and sacrificing ourselves like Jacinta for the conversion of sinners and the salvation of souls, we shall see holiness blossom among children, and the gradual perfecting of Christian life.

May it please God that shortly Jacinta be raised to the honor of the altar and that for this purpose, the process of her beatification may be commenced, for the good of souls and the greater glory of God and Our Lady of Fatima.

Act of Consecration

of the Human Race to
the Immaculate Heart of
Mary By Pope Pius XII

(The Holy Father urges all Catholics to consecrate themselves to the Immaculate Heart of Mary and to recite frequently this Act of Consecration, to which he has attached rich indulgences.)

Queen of the Most Holy Rosary, Refuge of the human race, Victress in all God's battles, we humbly prostrate ourselves before thy throne, confident that we shall receive mercy, grace and bountiful assistance and protection in the present calamity, not through our own inadequate merits, but solely through the great goodness of thy Maternal Heart.

To thee, to thy Immaculate Heart, in this, humanity's tragic hour, we consign and consecrate ourselves, in union not only with the Mystical Body of thy Son, Holy Mother Church, now in such suffering and agony in so many places and sorely tried in so many ways, but also with the entire world, torn by fierce strife, consumed in a fire of hate, victim of its own wickedness.

May the sight of the widespread material and moral destruction, of the sorrows and anguish of countless fathers and mothers, husbands and wives, brothers and sisters, and innocent children, of the great number of lives cut off in the flower of youth, of the bodies mangled in horrible slaughter, and of the tortured and agonized souls in danger of being lost eternally, move thee to compassion!

O Mother of Mercy, obtain peace for us from God, and above all procure for us those graces which prepare, establish and assure the peace.

Queen of Peace, pray for us and give to the world now at war the peace for which all peoples are longing, peace in the truth, justice and charity of Christ. Give peace to the warring nations and to the souls of men, that in the tranquillity of order the Kingdom of God may prevail.

Extend thy protection to the infidels and to all those still in the shadow of death; give them peace and grant that on them, too, may shine the sun of truth, that they may unite with us in proclaiming before the one and only Savior of the world, "Glory to God in the highest and peace to men of good will."

Give peace to the peoples separated by error or by discord, and especially to those who profess such singular devotion to thee and in whose home an honored place was ever accorded thy venerated image (today perhaps often kept hidden to await better days): bring them back to the one fold of Christ under the one true Shepherd.

Obtain peace and complete freedom for the Holy Church of God; stay the spreading flood of modern paganism; enkindle in the faithful the love of purity, the practice of the Christian life, and an apostolic zeal, so that the servants of God may increase in merit and in number.

Lastly, as the Church and the entire human race were consecrated to the Sacred Heart of Jesus, so that in reposing all hope in Him, He might become for them the sign and pledge of victory and salvation: so we in like manner consecrate ourselves forever also to thee and to thy Immaculate Heart, our Mother and Queen, that thy love and patronage may hasten the triumph of the Kingdom of God, and that all nations, at peace with one another and with God, may proclaim thee blessed and with thee may raise their voices to resound from pole to pole in the chant of the ever-lasting Magnificat of glory, love and gratitude to the Heart of Jesus, where alone they can find truth and peace. Amen.

Prayers
of the Angel

I

My God, I believe, I adore, I hope, and I love Thee. Pardon those who believe not, adore not, hope not, and love Thee not.

II

Most Holy Trinity, Father, Son, and Holy Ghost: I humbly adore Thee, I offer Thee the most precious Body, Blood, Soul, and Divinity of Our Lord Jesus Christ present in all the tabernacles of the world, in reparation for the outrages wherewith He Himself is offended. Through the infinite merits of His Most Sacred Heart and the intercession of the Immaculate Heart of Mary, grant me the conversion of sinners.

Prayer to the Immaculate Heart of Mary
To Obtain the Beatification of Jacinta Marto[14]

O Mary, who in thy maternal love hast chosen little Jacinta to be the confidante of thy Immaculate Heart so grieved by the sins of mankind, thou who didst inspire her with a great spirit of penance, an ardent zeal for the conversion of sinners, and an intense desire to repair the blasphemies against thy Immaculate Conception, vouchsafe, we humbly beseech thee, to obtain from the most merciful Heart of Jesus the grace of being elevated to the honor of the altars, the saintly little girl,

---

14 As evidence that the good God does hear the prayers of the faithful, Saints Jacinta and Francisco were canonized on May 13, 2017 by Pope Francis.

who, having been the object of thy predilection, thou hast given us as a model of apostolate and reparation. Amen.

Say this Prayer after each
decade of the Rosary

"O, my Jesus, forgive us our sins. Save us from the fire of hell! Lead all souls to heaven, especially those in need of your mercy.

Hymn to
Our Lady of Fatima

1

Thou hast come, O loving Mother,
And didst rest upon a tree;
Deign to hear the humble praises
We, Thy children, sing to Thee.

(CHORUS)
Ave, ave, ave, Mother of the Lord.
Ave, ave, we all say of one accord.

2

Noonday brightness saw Thy coming
While the children said their beads:
In Thy mercy, Virgin Mary,
Be our help in these dire needs,

(CHORUS)

3

Shelter us beneath Thy mantle,
We are children of Thy love;

At the end of these great trials
Lead us to Thy Son above.

(CHORUS)

4

At Thy feet we ask a blessing
For this world and for us all;
Thou, the refuge of poor sinners,
Into Hell let us not fall.

(CHORUS)

5

For Thy name Thou hast selected
Lady of the Rosary;
Do grant peace to all the nations,
To our Country Victory.

(CHORUS)

 TAN·BOOKS

TAN Books is the Publisher You Can Trust With Your Faith.

TAN Books was founded in 1967 to preserve the spiritual, intellectual, and liturgical traditions of the Catholic Church. At a critical moment in history TAN kept alive the great classics of the Faith and drew many to the Church. In 2008 TAN was acquired by Saint Benedict Press. Today TAN continues to teach and defend the Faith to a new generation of readers.

TAN publishes more than 600 booklets, Bibles, and books. Popular subject areas include theology and doctrine, prayer and the supernatural, history, biography, and the lives of the saints. TAN's line of educational and homeschooling resources is featured at TANHomeschool.com.

TAN publishes under several imprints, including TAN, Neumann Press, ACS Books, and the Confraternity of the Precious Blood. Sister imprints include Saint Benedict Press, Catholic Courses, and Catholic Scripture Study.

**For more information about TAN,
visit TANBooks.com**

**Or call us toll-free at
(800) 437-5876**

TAN·CLASSICS

*A collection of the finest literature
in the Catholic tradition.*

978-0-89555-227-3

978-0-89555-154-2

978-0-89555-155-9

Our TAN Classics collection is a well-balanced sampling
of the finest literature in the Catholic tradition.

978-0-89555-230-3

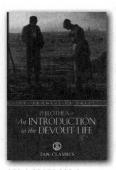

978-0-89555-228-0

978-0-89555-151-1

TAN·BOOKS

978-0-89555-153-5   978-0-89555-149-8   978-0-89555-199-3

The collection includes distinguished spiritual works of
the saints, philosophical treatises and famous biographies.

978-0-89555-226-6   978-0-89555-152-8   978-0-89555-225-9

Visit us at TANBooks.com

Spread the Faith with . . .

TAN·BOOKS

A Division of Saint Benedict Press, LLC

TAN books are powerful tools for evangelization. They lift the mind to God and change lives. Millions of readers have found in TAN books and booklets an effective way to teach and defend the Faith, soften hearts, and grow in prayer and holiness of life.

Throughout history the faithful have distributed Catholic literature and sacramentals to save souls. St. Francis de Sales passed out his own pamphlets to win back those who had abandoned the Faith. Countless others have distributed the Miraculous Medal to prompt conversions and inspire deeper devotion to God. Our customers use TAN books in that same spirit.

If you have been helped by this or another TAN title, share it with others. Become a TAN Missionary and share our life changing books and booklets with your family, friends and community. We'll help by providing special discounts for books and booklets purchased in quantity for purposes of evangelization. Write or call us for additional details.

TAN Books
Attn: TAN Missionaries Department
P.O. Box 410487
Charlotte, NC 28241

Toll-free (800) 437-5876
missionaries@TANBooks.com